*The Only Snow
in Havana*

The Only Snow in Havana

by
Elizabeth Hay

Cormorant Books

Published with the assistance of the Canada Council, the Ontario Arts Council, and the Government of Ontario through the Ministry of Culture and Communications.

Portions of this book first appeared in *The Capilano Review*, *Fiction International*, *Ikon*, and *Tessera*.

Front cover artwork is from an oil on canvas by Jean Hay, courtesy of the artist.

Published by Cormorant Books Inc.,
RR 1, Dunvegan, Ontario, Canada K0C 1J0.

Printed and bound in Canada.

Canadian Cataloguing in Publication Data

Hay, Elizabeth, 1951-
The only snow in Havana

ISBN 0-920953-80-8

I. Title.

PS8565 . A875065 1992   C818 ' .5407   C92-090453-X
PR9199 . 3 . H39065 1992

for Mark

CONTENTS

Snow and Fur Counterpoint

In the plaza the low stone benches were warm, the sound of clipping everywhere—hedges, hair. A man hoisted a load of flowers onto his back as a voyageur would have hoisted furs.

North elides into south. Hot into cool. Two avocados ripened on top of the fridge, two cold sores blossomed on my lips. Those connections were comforting because one thing slid into another and each was less alone.

I had gone to Mexico to get warm, and to leave my various northernisms behind: my seriousness, my caution, my smalltown self-consciousness and eagerness to please. In a letter from a friend the "i" in my name jumped above the line and she typed in brackets ('the captive "i" leaping free?'). A comment I brooded about.

On warm nights I read about Champlain, father of Canada, founder of the fur trade, "always travelling with an hungry heart with the great South Sea ever a day's journey in advance."

In *The Fur Trade* Harold Innis wrote about beaver fields; they sounded dark and fertile, the fur trade "in full bloom". Down the street a barber cut heads of thick hair and swept black flowers off the floor.

Innis wrote about a hard country combed for something soft: *castor gras, castor sec, castor gras d'été, demi-gras d'hiver, castor sec d'hiver*—a fur vocabulary as soft as the scurvied mouths of Champlain's men; they drew out their teeth with their fingers.

Champlain kept looking for comfort. He designed his first settlement as a plaza surrounded by buildings and shaded by a big elm. Ste-Croix, 1604. Houses, a storehouse, a handmill, a bakehouse, a cookhouse. That winter, snow fell on October 6th and stayed for six months.

There was engendered in the mouths of those who had scurvy large pieces of superfluous fungus flesh (which caused great putrefaction). . . the men could neither get up nor move, nor could they even be held upright without fainting away; so that of 79 of us, 35 died, and more than 28 were very near it.

Winter made Champlain eloquent about summer. He noted the appearance and progress of every green thing: cherry buds, spring primroses, raspberries and herbs, white violets, chervil and sorrel. He made a garden in a meadow, surrounded it with ditches stocked with trout, "arranged a summerhouse with fine trees", and sat there listening to the birds.

Even after sixteen years in Canada, Champlain still believed in an easy passage to the China seas. His maps of Canada look like French parks dotted with plump trees—slides of yearning between wilderness and home.

What are the sensibilities of a country founded on something as ambivalent as fur?

"We flew into northern Quebec," a fur buyer in Toronto told me, "and when we had lunch the chief came in with a big roasting pan. He took off the lid and went around the table showing each of us. It was a freshly skinned beaver, a quivering mass, with the tail alongside."

"Quivering?"

"Every animal twitches when it's freshly killed."

"What colour was the flesh?"

"Dark red. Almost a bluish red."

"And the tail alongside?"

"The tail is some kind of delicacy."

Delicate beavertails instead of silk. Champlain had hoped for Cathay. Instead, he pursued a dark and mobile crop through the snow, trapping animals and wearing them. Animal skins become our own skin, swinging emptily and apologetically.

It was a warm summer morning. I caught the streetcar at Yonge and King, rode under green maples to Spadina (that long wide street lined with fur outlets and Chinese restaurants) and walked into winter. Whites, greys, blacks, browns. The season they were trapped.

Two tiers of furs went from the floor to the ceiling. The vault was dark and cold. A forest after a fire, all the animals were gone.

I brushed against a black mink and it swung back and forth. "They're warm because they breathe," the furrier said.

That night I sat on the verandah and wore the smell of apple trees, the soft death of insects and grass. Fruit fell and animals fell and summer moved away as beautifully as a fur coat.

In Harold Innis's first year at university he got so lonely that by Christmas he decided to quit. His family persuaded him not to, and, pulling his work around him, he continued. *The Fur Trade* is the most detailed economic history ever written about Canada.

Innis spent ten years compiling his delighted list of facts: the average weight of a beaver is fifty-five pounds, the average weight of a beaver pelt is one and a half to two pounds, the farther north the darker the fur, the colder the winter the thicker the fur. He made lists of what traders paid: a fathom of small blue beads for a beaver robe, a small brass kettle for sixty marten, four peppercorns for a beaver skin.

In 1924 he canoed from the Peace River to Great Slave Lake and then took a river steamer down the Mackenzie River to Aklavik. He started his work on the fur trade by making himself familiar with the look of it. That summer his limp disappeared.

His economic history made me think about emotional history, a book that would chart the emotional underpinnings of Canada and show how our longing for warmth was fulfilled.

A very handsome man called me.

"Are you writing?" he asked.

"About fur. I'm not sure why. Partly having lived in Yellowknife, the cold and people trapping. But I suspect it's mostly sexual, can you enlighten me?"

He didn't call back.

In a fur shop on King Street all the women sewed by hand, and all the men used machines. The men had fluff on their shoulders. Hairs settled on a half-eaten plum.

"Don't look at the pictures," the furrier told me as we walked past calendars of naked women. "The boys love them."

"It's all sex," he said. "Frenchmen believed beaver had a lot of potency and if they wore beaver hats it would increase their own. You see," he said, "castoreum is the liquid inside a beaver's scent glands. If you go up to Mistassini in northern Quebec, Indians still make a brew out of them and drink it to make them virile. They have to make it fresh each time, and they pour what's left over into a hollow tree trunk. One night we were watching a movie in the community hall and we heard this howling on the other side of the bay. The dogs had been drinking the leftovers in the tree trunk and now they were tearing across the bay, crazy with lust."

When I grew accustomed to the light in the vault the furs looked like soft ghosts.
"How do you clean them?" I asked the owner.
"Like your hair," he said. "We take sawdust damp-ened with a solvent and hand-rub the garment. The sawdust is like a face cloth and we use it gently, and hand-comb the fur and brush it so the sawdust gets to the bottom. It's like dampening your hair and using a soft brush."
He gave me a page from a book called "Commodity Storage Requirements". Fur comes after Dates and before Grapes and Honey. Warm things surround it. In Mexico they surround the dead with food.
"How did you find me?" he asked.
I found him in the Yellow Pages, where furs are listed after funeral.

In the plaza in Mexico City, with the sun on my back and lizards on the palm trees, and an ice-cream store just beyond, thoughts of snow drifted in. Fat flakes. Tangible cold.
Snow and fur have that in common—two forms of ambivalent softness.
On Sunday I went to mass. During the service people talked, children played, a boy walked down the aisle with two balloons. They seemed to feel safe and relaxed under the image of Christ on the cross. Comfort acquired through pain.
Innis includes David Thompson's description: *The houses of the Beaver were pierced through, the Dams cut through, and the water of the Ponds low-*

*ered, or wholly run off, and the houses of the Beaver
and their Burrows laid dry, by which means they
became an easy prey to the Hunter.*

Snow is the white backdrop against which animals
panic, the calm landscape in which traps are set.

Fur travels. Snow is still. The bleak and sensual
point to which we return, our sense of worth always melting.

Snow appears simple and isn't. It's cold and warm,
light and dark, soft and hard. Snow is solid but it flows, fur
is continuous but composed of millions of hairs. Fur is warm
and dark and soft. It wraps us against death and wraps us in
death. Sensual violence, we wear it casually—the luxury of
warmth, the memory of the trap. We can smell ambivalence,
bury our fingers in it, an object on a hanger—beautiful,
lonely, empty of its owner.

Stan used to tear along the shore of Great Slave Lake
and shimmy on his back in the snow—a dog who introduced
me to a world where shedding happens inevitably but not
completely. In the mornings I found traces of him on the
sofa, shedding himself into our memories.

"Stan died," Keith said over the phone from Toronto.
Keith and I were separated but still married.

We shed things and are left with ourselves, our soft
sorrow at the way our lives are.

* * *

Sweet ruin of a spoonful of sugar in coffee. Melting snow is
a northern ruin, in the south civilizations melt.

We saw Tulum in the rain. A ruin in ruined weather.
The guide pointed out the temple to the Mayan god of the
honeybee. Until the Conquest, Mexico didn't have sugar;
then Cortes lingered on, permeating everything.

In Mérida we sat at a table outside the hotel, granules

of sugar under our fingertips. We stirred sugar into our coffee and noticed the absence of flowers, the pruned trees, the benches lopsided and partially gone. The long sigh of cushions being sat upon.

I kept thinking about the way things disappear. The way things that aren't here are: sugar in coffee, people in our lives. "Think of blue," Keith used to say when I couldn't sleep.

Indians in white pillowcase shirts fell asleep over their small piles of mangoes and candies. So tired. The ruin of a ruined sleep.

Things leave us and we leave them, and then we try to catch up again. Snow and fur provide a pathway—snow to sugar, fur to coffee, north to south. They offer the texture and companionship of images and ideas.

The first time I saw Alec he was sitting next to an older woman at a language school in Cuernavaca, their heads bent in conversation. During the class he taught, I sat two rows back and listened to his Boston accent. I tried to see through his shirt and count the hairs on his chest.

Alec was translating things then. "Everything we say means six things," he said, implying that it takes a while for all six to penetrate.

I walked down the street near the school and turned back when the fragrance registered. Gardenias—ten feet away; a girl was selling little bouquets of six apiece. As she raised the small white handful to her face the image of Keith rose up. Something he had written about himself—my face rose over the back seat of the car like a harvest moon—writing a long time ago about his enormous self-consciousness, the light of which still trails me around.

I fell in love with Alec and followed him to Mexico City. I

moved into the house he shared with several friends, and immediately felt lost because I didn't have a life of my own, at least not enough of one.

One day I met a woman he had always been attracted to. She and her husband invited us for dinner, and Alec couldn't stop looking at her. Nor could I. She wiped the corners of her eyes with her fingertip, wiped her fingertip on a paper napkin, and left a black smear. While it was still light she closed the curtains, producing the same amount of duskiness as around her eyes. Lancôme. I had noticed the jars in the bathroom.

"Why didn't anything happen?" I asked him later.

"Well, she was married, for one thing."

She kissed her husband in the doorway, her blonde face leaning into his long black hair. He had been away in France for three years and only just come back.

After we had coffee she took us to eat the best hot-fudge sundaes in Mexico City. The place was Chiandoni's, on the corner of Pennsylvania and San Antonio. We sat at a small table with a mural of Venice on one wall and the Tower of Pisa on the other, and she talked about ego-permeability. People from mainland countries, she said, hug their identities to themselves and resist being permeated by new things. People from islands know how to be open to the world and learn languages quickly. She was from Iceland; her Spanish was perfect.

When she talked her husband looked away as though uninterested. When he talked it was to give her advice, and her face went hard. Over the hot-fudge sundaes she slipped her hand into his, and talked about being in Montreal in January, having hitchhiked through the snow and arrived at carnival time.

I asked Alec what he thought.

"The amazing thing is that they could be apart for

three and a half years and not fall in love with someone else."

I was quiet. An island of jealousy. Or, since I was impermeable to anything else, a mainland.

I asked Alec what he liked about me.

"Your eyebrows," he said.

I dreamt that Alec and I kept going back and forth each day to a swimming-hole. We would walk, and it seemed that his interest in me was flagging, and that it was always dark. I was imagining how to make love to him while we swam, when we turned around and saw a car stuck in deep snowdrifts. We went over to help, Alec in a swimsuit, and this the middle of winter. I said, "*¿Necesitas ayuda?*", do you need help? And the woman smiled. She was an Eskimo. So then we pushed the car, Alec in a parka and boots, but he wasn't Alec, he was Keith.

I woke up very sad.

In the small park which faced our house—a park of calla lilies, pruned bushes and palm trees—I leaned against a wall in the sun and asked, "The yellow trumpet-flower over there, do you know the English name?"

"Is there a flower called Cup of Gold?" Alec answered.

"With a coconut fragrance?"

"Yes, probably."

Cup of Gold. His long slim hands were dry; it was the dry season. We walked to the square and sat in an open café, the treetops shrieking with birds, and talked about healing. Homeopathy: like with like. An element, he said, plant or mineral, spun and diluted in purified water, produces the same symptoms as the illness, intensifying it so that the body is forced to throw it off. He had been sick for several months and gone to a homeopathic doctor as a last resort.

We sat at a table where the traffic curved; it got dark and the birds hushed. Like with like, he said. I thought of putting snow on frostbite, or butter on a burn, equally bad. Hot on hot, cold on cold, when what we want is cool on hot, and warm on cold. It got cooler as we talked. Under the streetlight his shirt was very white, like a loose bandage, or snow.

Evening turned the square into an underexposed photograph, yellowish, slightly off, as though we were already back home and projected on the wall.

Rose petals on wet cement. After the rain—sudden, quick, sparse. I read in my snow house, confined by the patio's four white walls, my books on a white wrought-iron table. One of the first phrases in my Spanish text was *la nieve es fria y blanca,* snow is cold and white.

Soft Spanish voices inside (dinner was cooking, the smells), the occasional clatter of a leaf falling hard, heavy— a small animal—from the magnolia tree above.

Alec rubbed his chalky hands together and bent over his notes, preparing on foolscap his classes about Mexican history: a complete civilization subjugated, the Indians demeaned, Mexicans went from reactionary to radical to reactionary with no clear motive beyond a search for identity.

At dusk we walked along the lip of the gorge, and he said that the word for dusk in Paraguay means mouth of night.

"What does Canada mean?" he asked. And I couldn't tell him.

"Canada has a crisis of too little identity," I said, "and Mexico has a crisis of too much."

"That would make an interesting story."

"You mean the comparison?"

"Yes."

Mexicans: polite and contained. Canadians, equally so. But Mexicans have pride, and Canadians don't. A slur sums it up. La Malinche was a Tlaxcalan princess captured by the Aztecs, sold into slavery to the Mayans, and presented to Cortes as a gift; she became the main strategist for the Conquest. Today, a Malinche is anyone who prefers foreigners to Mexicans. And since that preference runs deep throughout Mexico, she symbolizes their ambivalence towards outsiders, and, finally, their distaste for themselves.

But Mexicans don't belittle themselves, at least not to strangers. And they remember their past, while Canadians forget.

Frida Kahlo put empty dresses in her paintings to remind us of the wounded body that wasn't there. She was eighteen when the accident happened: a streetcar collided with her bus and in the impact a metal bar skewered her pelvis and fractured her spine.

We went to her house, a blue house behind a blue wall, in a cobblestoned section of Mexico City. The rooms had blue and yellow tiles, blue and yellow furniture, big paper flowers, life-size papier-mâché skeletons, a gaily painted body cast. In the last years of her life she could paint only by lying on her back in bed and looking at the mirror above.

Fur coats smell slightly of the animal. (The vault was dark because light damages fur. And cold. There was a wintry smell, and slight perfume; both bodies were missing.)

Six of her dresses hung in a glass case, empty but still smelling of her.

In Mexico flowers are wounds; crucifixes have floral stigmata.

A woman sells a few vegetables on the sidewalk. Radishes, scrubbed and shining, are arranged in a pyramid close to her brown hand, close to the hem of her purple dress. She has nothing else to sell, she couldn't be poorer, and yet she looks beautiful.

Canadian history makes the same unsettling point but in a more sombre way, because snow and fur are restrained. The most painful wounds can be rather lovely.

On Easter Sunday Alec and I go into a cathedral and Christ is laid out under a sheet on a long table, his head and feet exposed, a noose around his neck. I ask why growing up with this image doesn't make it harder to inflict pain. It seems to make it easier.

"Maybe not to inflict pain," Alec answers, "but to accept it."

We walk past five bouquets of red gladioli towards the front of the church, where an old woman kneels with a candle, her hand covered in wax as thick and white as bread dough—Christ rising.

* * *

Champlain married an eleven-year-old girl. He wrote six volumes about his life and didn't mention her once. For a long time I didn't even know her name.

Braids are fastened to a wall in a church, and I ask a woman knitting at the door; "When someone is sick," she answers, "they cut off a piece of their hair and put it on the wall, to be cured."

The hair is tacked to pieces of red velvet on the wall near the altar, soft blood on young thighs. I had been thinking about the way fur turns into words, an eleven-year-old's muffled no.

In 1599, eighty years after the Conquest, Champlain visited Mexico, and the city was still beautiful, "superbly

constructed of splendid temples, palaces and fine houses."
Four years later he went to Canada and dreamed about
Cathay. Every pelt he handled was a secondary pleasure. He
looked for a soft and fertile country, he found an eleven-year-
old girl. Beaver fields that men plough.

Out of respect for her age the marriage wasn't
consummated for two years, and in the third year she ran
away. Her parents denounced her publicly in Paris on
January 10th, 1614, alleging that

ever since her marriage, and especially since 1 Oct.
last, she had distressed them by fleeing from her
home, breaking her promise to live in amity with and
obedience to her husband. Neither he nor they could
locate her. . . .

Rather than eleven, historians say she was not yet
twelve. I suppose that makes her seem older and Champlain
less to blame. He was forty-three.

She was brought back against her will, and disinher-
ited by her parents.

It snowed heavily on the day she and Champlain signed their
marriage contract, December 27th, 1610. Hélène Boullé.
Her signature on the dowry document is "that of a little girl
whose fingers have not yet mastered the pen". Less than
three months later Champlain sailed for Canada. When he
came back he brought her beaded moccasins, and baskets of
sweet-grass decorated with porcupine quills.

The marriage was consummated at the beginning of
1613. In the spring Champlain left again for Canada. That
fall he returned and her *injures atroces et scandaleuses*
began. Three months later she ran away, and Champlain
filed a complaint with the police. How they found her, or
where, doesn't seem to be known.

When she was twenty-two she came out to Canada

with him and stayed four years. The final year was a starving one; by spring only four barrels of flour were left.

A painting shows her arrival at Quebec. She and Champlain are standing in an ox-drawn cart surrounded by settlers. What looks like snow must be daisies because it's summer. *Arrival of Madame Champlain* at Quebec is stored in the Public Archives of Canada. An imaginary rendering, it was painted long after they died.

Invisible in the painting is the mirror she wore on a chain at her waist. The Indians loved to peer into it. In their eyes she apparently became something of a goddess. She learned how to speak Algonquin (something Champlain never attempted to do) and taught them catechism. They would have preferred to worship her—so historians say.

When Champlain died in 1635 she was only thirty-six years old. She opened a convent, and as a foundress was allowed to have a fire in her room, a lay-sister to attend to her, and an undisturbed sleep. The others had to rise at four in the morning.

I watched a nun once, in southern Mexico. She sat on the edge of her bed on the other side of the room and brushed her waist-long hair two hundred times before putting it up.

Is that the image Hélène Boullé had of herself? Combing her life for something soft?

* * *

Quiet Toronto. Under a plum tree, full of small green plums, we talk about a man from Nicaragua who took the train from Toronto to Kingston and became entranced with the light; evening, he said, went on for ever. Long indirect rays; northern light is a slanting Cathay.

On Spadina the two obsessions are laid out: red and yellow signs with Chinese characters, seedy and subdued storefronts with furs in the windows. Where fur and Cathay finally meet.

The Iroquois name for ginseng, *garent-oguen*, has the same meaning as the Chinese: man's thigh. Outside an igloo Charles Hall picked up his brass sextant with bare hands, and burned his fingertips. At home my nephew plays with a hockey game, and in lieu of lost counters uses cloves.

One explorer tasted Cathay. In the coldest winter he ever experienced (1797, Reindeer Lake; no water was seen along the shore until July 5th), David Thompson watched herds of deer lying down for a few hours on the ice "as if to cool themselves". He killed a doe and plunged his freezing hands into the hot blood, only to wrench his hands away because the blood scalded his skin. Astonished, he examined the stomach and found it full of white moss, then traced the deer to where they had been feeding, "took a small piece, about the size of a nutmeg", and swallowed it. It burned in his stomach like "a coal of fire". Northern plants, Thompson concluded, have a "warm nature" which enables animals not only to bear the intense cold, but to find it warm.

Thirty-six years later, on August 15th, George Back observed the fur trade "in full bloom" on the shores of Great Slave Lake: "a few roses yet in bud, the colour of which was a deeper red than that of the roses which grow more south". The farther north, the darker the buds; in a mild climate marten have yellowish fur; in the cold—nearly black.

In a friend's garden in Toronto we eat strawberries from a bowl, fingering them in the dark summer night—a fur coat of sorts.

The Arctic used to be warm. Forty million years ago it was moist, treed, temperate, wrapped in mild weather of which fur is the vestige. Coal still bears the imprint of tropical leaves.

A soothing thought—to know that under so much cold lies the buried story of warmth.

"I remember my father's big fur coat," my mother said, "which he wore when he drove the horse for a funeral. The collar was otter, the coat light brown, and the buffalo robe over his knees dark, almost a black brown."

During the 1919 flu epidemic (the year my mother was born) her father buried so many people that he didn't get to bed for two weeks. He would come home, bathe, dress, lie down for a rest, and then go back to work—to the furniture store crammed with things someone might need, and the funeral parlour full of loss.

He died when my mother was seven, and her life (founded on warmth suddenly removed) entered a period of vulnerability and solitude.

She had always held his hand while she ate. Before bedtime he would wash her hands and dry each finger individually, then give her one hundred somersaults into bed. "And always as his foot reached the landing on the staircase, 'Daddy, I want a drink of water.' And back up he would come and get it for me."

After he died the only warmth she found was halfway up the stairs, where a hot-air register offered a comfortable place to sit.

Coffee spills out under the lid and burns my fingers: a coffee and chocolate-glazed from Titan Donuts on Sherbourne Street. I open *One Hundred Years of Solitude* and read the first line. "Many years later, as he faced the firing squad, Colonel Aureliano Buendía was to remember that distant afternoon when his father took him to discover ice."

In the heat of the moment to remember something so cold. In the heat of Colombia to begin a book with ice. If we were to begin a northern story with a similar object of allure, what would it be?

Something warm. Glenn Gould's hands in gloves
even in summer.

"Where are you swimming to?" Alec calls to me. "China?"

Explorers came looking for silks and found the
underhair of animals, soft and silky—China to the touch.

We find warmth indirectly: the imprint of redwood
leaves on arctic coal, the feel of a towel on my mother's
fingers. We reach the east by sailing west, arrive in China by
way of Yellowknife, that indirect route along yellow silk,
home.

The Only Snow in Havana

Alec and I leave Mexico soon after the earthquake. I continue to write about fur, smooth surfaces, in the midst of rubble. A baby buckles inside me.

As infants are pulled alive from the ruins of hospitals, we pack up death: the skeleton mask, the sugar skull with "Alec" written on its forehead, the paper cutout of Death with a scythe in its hands, the papier-mâché skeleton with a baseball cap and a grin. One baby is removed from his dead mother's arms, still alive and suckling.

I knock the scissors off the table. They hit the tiny sugar coffin on the shelf below and amputate the arms of the sugar corpse. I pick them up off the floor, reminded of a battle between the English and the French on Hudson Bay after which arms were found on the ice.

Images ripple south and north, find each other, keep each other company, fall in love.

In that moment before heat touches something frozen. One winter when I lived in Yellowknife, we entered a friend's cabin and all the plants were green, upright, perfect. It was -35° outside and, by accident, the oil stove had been left off all day. We turned it on and the plants collapsed.

Alec fingers a Brazilian song on his guitar and tells me the story of the movie *Black Orpheus*: the beautiful girl with long braids who falls in love with Orpheus and is chased by Death and caught during Carnival.

Alec says that a part of you dies when you move. He's been here so long his friends expected him to stay for ever. I'll spirit him away, I say to myself. I won't look back.

Bakeries begin to sell *pan de muertos*, fat sugared loaves decorated with crossbones for the Day of the Dead. It's early October. We fly to Canada—tears in Alec's eyes as the plane takes off, tell me again, why are we leaving?— and at home I fall asleep in that room I know so well and dream about a bogeyman who wears a skull mask and skull-and-crossbones necklace. As I wake up the mask and necklace melt; they're made of fat. In that moment of melting the monster becomes a gentle defender, and I wake up feeling oddly blessed.

Large hard flakes break against the windows. Beethoven on the radio, a brilliant improviser, they say, always altering his compositions. Weather improvises too. Soft/crisp. Deaf snow.

"What animals live here?"

"Owls," I answer.

Walking through the park. Snow, snow, snow. Murmur of my mother counting stitches not quite under her breath. We see two otters swimming inside their fenced enclosures, poking out their heads as the baby so far has refused to do. Snow stays on our faces and throws off the same amount of light as a streetlamp in Havana.

We went there on a last holiday before heading north, and found an eaten-away city full of peeling paint, falling petals, moths: no traffic, no American cars, no fashions in the windows, almost no commerce.

Un frozzen, they call soft ice cream, the rapidly

melting yet static past.

"Let's stay," said Alec, and I smiled. "You'd get used to the lineups in a month."

"Never."

The old story: he loved anything Latin, I wanted snow.

We found a bust of Christopher Columbus under a ceiba tree, a chandelier over a public garden, a long seawall to walk along. We waited in line, washed with small nameless bars of soap, argued about love.

How do you describe that pain? Of Alec waking up, still lethargic from his mysterious illness which hung on and on, and of my starting.

"Are you sick?"

He shrugged.

"I'm tired of this, Alec."

"What?"

"I'm tired of this—of your being tired. This isn't what I want."

I wanted to make love, mid-afternoon, hot, a cross-breeze through the windows, and we did, but he was too tired to be interested.

"Is it because you're still sick?"

"I don't know any more. It's been so long. I don't know what it's like to feel completely well. I don't know if I'm sick here or here." And he pointed to his body, and then his head.

I imagined nursing a man as well as a child, being stuck with a man because we were having a child.

"I want to feel loved," I said.

"I've thought that too. That I don't love you the way you love me."

"I don't know how I love you now. Probably the way you love me. Half-hearted."

"I'm laughing," he said, "but it isn't funny."

We walked up the driveway to Hemingway's house, recognizing it from the movie *Memories of Underdevelopment.* The underdevelopment of love. A black girl slipped out of the trees and asked us something in a dialect we didn't understand.

Switching to Spanish, "Aren't you Russian?" she asked.

Through the windows we saw the long graceful necks of antelopes and gazelles, a collection of sheathed daggers, a rack of huge shoes, and on the wall in the bathroom a running account of his weight as it went dangerously down.

A woman's voice drew us to a bar on the corner. Empty glasses of cane liquor covered her table, and a man with a guitar sat beside her. They sang for pleasure. Long earrings, low-cut sleeveless blouse; she raised her arm and talcum powder shone in her armpit, the only snow in Havana.

I dreamt about Keith again. In the dream I decided to go back to him, there didn't seem to be any alternative.

Afterwards we went to the beach, the soft sea. Alec immediately made friends. I sat to one side and choked back tears, so unsure whether this was the life I wanted. The baby was my ticket home, the only thing that could have persuaded Alec to leave Mexico. And that in itself was all wrong, that I should be so responsible for his emotional upheaval, his sadness about leaving.

In the afternoon we agreed we would try to make it work. In the evening, walking down a dark street—how?

"If you could be more enthusiastic about us," I said.

"If you could be more enthusiastic about life," he said.

I shook a towel over the balcony and Alec's bathing suit fell out, twelve storeys, down to the bottom of crumbling Havana, a crumbling relationship. Then a falling city—Mexico. We walked into the lobby and all the Mexicans on our tour were weeping. Calling, calling, trying to get news. Neither elevator worked. We climbed twelve flights.

A day later, a second earthquake, and the prospect that buildings would keep on falling.

As soon as planes were allowed to land we flew back. We walked along Monterrey, then Insurgentes, wearing masks through the dust. Someone told Alec about a man trapped under a collapsed building who survived by drinking his urine.

"How did he collect it?"

"In his hands, probably."

Imagining the contortions of mouth to penis.

It was dark. People were in the streets selling under a half-moon, eating, talking, skirting buildings which looked like cakes whose layers had slid off. I made a comment about how remarkable it was, the normality that coexisted with tragedy, and Alec gave me a look—impatient, hostile, uninterested—which hurt into the night. With all the tension of the earthquake (on television we had seen, by way of a lowered camera, people still alive in a building) and all the tension of our move, and of us.

* * *

Snow is falling. In the park a rope of fragile flakes hangs suspended between two twigs. The baby settles inside me. A new world, created from a particle of mud and the body of a loon.

I read about Champlain. In the absence of silk and spices he and de Monts took back a six-month-old moose calf, and a number of caribou. They gave them to the king, who turned them loose at Saint-Germain, where they died for lack of water "or other commodities".

I read about Indians taken to France who died within the year. I make notes, filling pages with anxiety: waiting to spot land, looking for signs—feathers on the sea, grass, a rush of water between my legs.

Large hands, lips like Alec's. I forget she's a girl, seeing him. After her bath we dust her with talcum powder.

Snow builds up on the balcony, four feet high. Everyone notices the changes in the baby except me. Her eyes are more alert, they say, she looks around much more. Stronger too, my brother says, and bigger.

She changes like the snow. I didn't realize how high it was becoming, only how high it became.

Puritan Cathay

Billie Holiday's voice
teeters like small bound feet,
the way she sings "baaa—by".

My daughter plays with her toes.
I write about Cathay.

Salem. Unnatural quiet. Almost no seagulls, no smell of the sea. We bring a lamp into the kitchen and it makes the overhead light less lonely.

We're new.

The town of A, the scarlet letter, the beginning. And such a sad beginning: Hester Prynne blinked in the unaccustomed sunlight, my daughter's hand in mine.

I read *Robinson Crusoe* in the doughnut shop. The waitress bends her bleached head forward—mauve lips, fins of an old Buick.

"They grow so fast," looking at my daughter. "My baby is thirty-five."

The next time she doesn't remember us.

"She doesn't remember us," I say to Alec.

"She's just pretending not to."

The third time I go in she says, "You were in twice before. Is it a boy or a girl?"

Donut Cove. A seaside doughnut shop.

The party. We are all strangers overeager for friendship — the lack of conversation, the heartiness, the impossibility of finding music to suit the mood or change it.

One man flings his tie over his shoulder, trying to look casual in office clothes. His wife is cold. She puts on his suit jacket and hunches in her chair. He suggests she sit beside him on the sofa, and she shakes her head.

"You're not *that* cold." He laughs.

When she does sit beside him, exaggerating her coldness, looking much older than he does, he immediately gets up and sits in her chair. "My back needs a straight chair," slumping in it, "I'm getting old."

On the way home Alec says, "I miss my friends."

The photo. Alec is standing against a painted backdrop of flowers and a banner held aloft by two birds. On the banner, TE TRAIGO ESTAS FLORES. The photo is twelve years old. Alec is wearing summer trousers and sandals, a shoulder-bag, a wide-brimmed hat which he holds over his heart. "I bring you these flowers."

Skinny, scuffed but neat, serious, very young. A traveller. At the bottom of the photo a few strands of hair from the photographer's head blow into the picture.

Alec is Robinson Crusoe in reverse. Cast ashore on his native land, head bent over a computer manual, editing jargon to pay the rent. Crusoe taught a parrot how to say his name, Alec is taught how to parrot.

"He would sit upon my finger, and lay his bill close to my face, and cry, 'Poor Robin Crusoe! Where are you? Where have you been? How come you here?' And such things as I had taught him."

The afternoon sun comes into the laundromat and falls on a woman who is missing two lower teeth. My daughter's clothes are missing my daughter. I nuzzle her head and the side of her face, then watch her swirl emptily in the dryer.

An expedition has just reached the North Pole. One

of the party was evacuated three weeks early and his dog, remaining behind, died a day before they reached the Pole. From the paper I read out, "He never pulled well after his master left, and died of unknown causes."

"*Tristeza*," Alec says, "*se murió de tristeza*. There's nothing unknown about that."

He died of sadness.

A child cries one house over. In Mexico City we were always awakened at one in the morning as the child on the other side of the wall began to cry. The mother came in yelling, shut up, shut up, SHUT UP. . . .

"Murder, suicide or madness," Alec says. "Those are the alternatives."

I look at him, my glance accusing him of exaggeration once again.

"I don't mean you murder someone or kill yourself or go into a mental hospital. I mean you let parts of yourself die or you don't let parts of other people exist, or you go crazy."

In the rocking-chair, late at night, he smokes a Havana cigar, reads *The Quiet American*. He is the unquiet American.

"What did you dream about when you were a kid?" I ask him.

"I always dreamt about going away. My favourite fairytales were about people who walked over mountains and found something they had never known about."

And I realize that's why I fell in love with him.

He sits with our daughter in his lap and teaches her Spanish so he'll have somebody to talk to. "Where have you been? How come you here?"

* * *

We eat purple grapes. Stems pile up in the middle of the table; furs receded as settlements advanced.

Francis Parkman called his work of many volumes a history of the American forest. I think of leaves when I read the title; a history of leavetakings, sheddings, falling in and out of love.

If only I could be loyal enough. But what is enough? I must mean enough to kill any doubts before they arise. As if love can be reduced to loyalty.

"Don't worry," says Alec as I lie awake, "I may never hold a high-paying job but I'll earn enough."

He has a new ailment: any physical exertion, even a walk, and he breaks out in a rash so itchy that he runs into the coldest part of the apartment, stripping off clothes, trying to shed his detested American skin but unable to—trapped inside the contradiction of wanting warmth and not being able to have it.

Yesterday I realized how quiet he'd become. Visit after visit and he didn't talk.

"You know what it is? I'm not doing anything worth talking about. . . . And I don't think enough of myself to even talk about that."

No one ever asks him about where he's been. All those years away, and they have no curiosity; they get a certain small satisfaction from knowing he's back and floundering. They're ahead of him now.

In 1603, Champlain returned to France with an Iroquois woman and the son of a Montagnais chief. Nothing is known about the woman. The boy was baptized, dressed in a blue coat and bonnet and taken to the palace at Saint-Germain. There he played with the three-year-old Prince Louis, who was so pleased with his little "Canada" that he sent him dainties from his own table. Throughout the winter the boy sickened, and in June 1604 he died.

On Washington Street I notice a plaque— "pressed to death". Right where it happened a printing shop presses out copies. Giles Corey "broke charity" with his wife and she was hanged; others accused him of witchcraft and he was pressed to death; they used stones.

All our large and small disloyalties. Wharfs (silent now, not a ship in sight) reeked of cinnamon, cloves, nutmeg and tea. No one seems to remember where Gallow's Hill was.

Beside me in bed: "You know when Lea was talking about her father and her husband, how they couldn't get it together? I thought, is that what you think of me?"

"Why did you think I was thinking that?"

"I just thought it. Were you?"

"—No."

"You're lying."

Snow. A few flakes, a light dusting on roofs and street. Faster now. Big fat flakes.

On the cover of a college calendar a large house half-disappears into falling snow. Snow is so peaceful because it's uninterrupted. (Our daughter crying, again.)

The tension in the apartment—the lack of a job, all his doubts about being here. And what am I? The snow? Covering him over?

When I make a short trip to Canada he jokingly makes a *suplente*, a substitute woman. He drapes a Guatemalan skirt over the seat of the sofa, arranges an embroidered blouse over the back, runs a woven belt across the middle and a clay necklace around the neck. He sets the white skull mask on top and dangles an earring from its bony left ear.

My empty boots for feet.

We stay there, Death and I, for a month, until we have

a party and need the sofa to sit on.

* * *

Alec throws open every window and every door. He strings up the hammock on the verandah and, basking in the hot humid air, says he feels almost at home.

"What is the meaning of life?" he calls to me. I go out and find him swinging our daughter in the hammock. "Where does she come from?"

It starts to rain. Dozens of birds are suddenly noisy and the smell of dust is very strong.

"Where do you come from?" he asks her.

How come you here?

Yesterday, on the way to Boston, we passed a truck piled high with canoes, eight of them, drifting north. Such an odd sight amid the concrete—as were the flowering trees, which are so intricate and soft and beautiful. Persephone making her appearance.

Underground, a sugar coffin dissolves and our lives, sweetened, escape into blossom, new grass, leaves close to the window. The old smell lifts (slightly stale, crowded, warm: the Irish soda bread we made all winter and ate around the small table, Alec reading want ads, our daughter reaching for them). We celebrate by pulling the plastic off the windows and letting in a champagne of light.

Leaves surround the verandah, the verandah half-surrounds the house, and more houses (graceful, tall, beautiful houses) surround this one in a display of Puritan sensuality.

In the late eighteenth century Salem and Boston sent ships to China, and the China trade—echoed by Hester Prynne's "rich, voluptuous, Oriental characteristic"—began. They took ginseng from the cool woodlands of the

Atlantic seaboard, furs from Nootka Sound, opium from Turkey; they trafficked in immortality, death and forgetfulness.

In Canton, fur boats were met by flower boats whose upper works were carved with petals and birds. Low moans issued from painted windows and stirred the loins of every Yankee sailor.

One form of sensuality was traded for another. Fur (soft, silent) was traded for porcelain, "a clear ringing sound when struck, one could see the liquid contained" between parted thighs. Fur became translucent and fragrant, cinnamon and silk. One thing became another.

Salem became Cathay. Po Adam, the wealthiest merchant of Quallah Battoo, thought Salem was a country in itself, and "one of the richest and most important sections of the globe."

In the museum we look at displays of porcelain, model ships, lacquered tea-tables.

A bamboo and cane ottoman with a beautiful sloping line. A sofa.

Vases.

A gaming table in black and gold lacquer with mother-of-pearl inlay.

A sewing table with ivory fittings—spools, needles.

An ivory fan.

In silver: a praying mantis, nutmeg grater, hand-held vase.

Light comes through the window, brushes against a fern, reclines in the ottoman, lies on the sofa. We leave.

After twenty years in Canton, J.P. Cushing came back with an ivory ball consisting of twenty patterned and perforated spheres carved one within the other. The outside ball was carved first, and through those holes the next ball, on and on—deeper and deeper into ivory—in a process of looking for Cathay and finding intricate, infinitely beautiful, unbelievable white. A snowball from China.

After supper we go down to Palmer Cove and sit on the seawall in a long sweep of golden light. We listen to cowbells—halyards jostling against masts, a pasture of sailboats, the quiet lapping of grass.

"Was having the baby the biggest change in your life?" I ask Alec.

"Meeting you was a pretty big change."

My disbelief. But he repeats it. "I'm learning how to love you."

* * *

The patience of snow. Carving twenty balls of memory.

Musk-oxen graze on sweet coltsfoot, mountain sorrel, lousewort, pendant grass, water sedge. Originally they came from the high plains of northern China.

J.P. Cushing often wore Chinese robes in his mansion in Boston. Musk-ox hair sweeps the ground.

At the head of a lane beyond Gloucester we notice a plaque to Champlain. "Due east from here on July 16, 1605 the Sieur de Monts sent Samuel de Champlain ashore to parley with some Indians. They danced for him and traced an outline map of Massachusetts Bay. These French explorers named this promontory 'The Cape of Islands'."

Champlain—convinced he was close to Cathay.

* * *

Smell of incense and popcorn (the popcorn man from Alec's childhood). On the raised outdoor platform a long table is set with two vases of spring flowers, a bowl of fruit, and incense.

The Buddhist master rings a bell and invites the gods to bless the new Asian wing of the Peabody Museum.

A tall, lean, aristocratic Yankee introduces Vice-Consul Choo, stoops low to wave at him eight feet away, then introduces "Mrs. Wang, uh, Wong."

In the Chinese mind fur was the ultimate luxury: the lustre and warmth of a cold land.

"Where are you swimming to? China?"

Unmapped. The long way around. Every arrival is a surprise. In the museum I come upon a floating raven in a glass case, and suddenly recognize where I am.

We go down the steps past the wild rose and down to the sea, carrying the perfume with us—wild roses everywhere.

Our daughter licks pebbles, Alec reads García Márquez out loud: the doctor and Fermina, spending their first night together, talk for hours. He touches her neck with the *yemas*, yolks, of his fingertips, his penis *enarbolado*, treelike, in all its leafy eagerness. I listen, lose track of the Spanish, start thinking about our neighbour Jean, the shyest man I've ever met, and how he married Joanie.

He was working at a gas station where she went to fill up her car. One day she overheard his name, and sent a card to "Jean, at the gas station". Inside, "You think you're nobody special but you must be to get this card." Signed "Guess who?" A couple of weeks later she drove up for gas, and just as she was about to pull out she leaned out the window and called to him, "Get any mail lately?"

He asked her out and two months later they were married.

The doctor didn't love her, Alec is reading, but that night he felt there was no obstacle to their inventing a good love.

The tide goes out along this coastline of rosehips,

lilies and woodland, the warmth of the sun untropical but penetrating. We bend to smell hedges of wild roses, hardly having to bend, intoxicated by northern sensuality: a special coastline of white flesh marked off by brown—the lovely milkiness of breasts, crotch, underarms—where a benign sort of winter resides. We cup our hands around the soft wreckage of snow, inventing warmth.

In 1606, Marc Lescarbot reached the new world. "There came from the land odours incomparable for sweetness, brought with a warm wind so abundantly that all the Orient parts could not produce greater abundance. We did stretch out our hands as it were to take them, so palpable were they."

That first summer he planted herbs and grains, explored the banks of the Annapolis River, exulted in finding wild grapes as big as plums "and so black that where their juice was spilt they left a stain."

Evenings, he read in his room or wrote about the "subtle" beaver, and snow, "that cloak of fur". Of Indian ceremonies for the dead—"they are accustomed to make their lamentations for a long period of days, of about a month . . . weepings and cryings. . . ."

I listen to the door opening and closing downstairs. So quiet. Muted. A phone call. And is it Joanie crying?

Has she lost the baby?

"After our savages had wept for Panoniac they went to the place where his cabin stood while he was alive, and there burnt all that he had left . . . to the end that none should quarrel over his succession."

Jean had a bouquet of flowers (we met him on the sidewalk) and he kept bending his face down to the tallest pink one to smell it, smiling as he told us how sick she was.

When we moved to Salem, Jean was the first person we met. He knocked on the door of our second-floor apartment and presented us with two cans of beer and a toy rabbit. He was bashful and quickly backed away. They were excited about our baby, and wanted one of their own.

We had a party and invited them. Jean stood by the door and, halfgrinning, halflooking away, asked, "Do you have any pictures of Mexican pyramids? I don't know why but I'm fascinated by ruins." His burst of laughter, his ruined teeth. He said nothing else all night.

There's a Canadian for you, I said to Alec. Jean's parents moved down from Quebec forty years ago.

Explorers discovered softness, "their gums quite putrid, and legs as big round as their bodies." To soothe the baby, teething now for two days, I put on "Without Your Love", Billie Holiday's old child's voice.

The radio plays an interview with her recorded in 1956. "I used to think I couldn't sing without gardenias in my hair, so a friend of mine sent me six gardenias, and they had put these pins in them to go on your dress and I didn't take the pin out, and I stuck it in my head and I didn't even realize, and I got on stage and it was a good thing I had on a black dress with a high neck cause the blood was running all down my dress. . . ."

Soft stoned voice, eaten away by emotion. Jezebel —only the palms remain—jazz.

In the park people silently, all by themselves, cook in the sun. Turn the colour of loneliness. Red, painfully aware of itself, the scarlet of Hester Prynne's letter.

Cool fragrance after three days of rain. I pick up the paper at seven, surprised at how the coolness is shot through with warmth.

What are the smells? Settled dust, and growing leaves. The sea. The coming rain, the heat that's over, the lilacs long gone.

Keith's parents come to visit. We walk to Hawthorne's house and they take a picture of my daughter and me under the sign, in the shadow of Hester and Pearl.

They are so kind, so genuinely fond, that in my gratitude after their departure, my flurry of emotion and memory, I phone Keith and stumble over his name—Alec, I call him, horrified to hear it slip out.

"No, that's the other guy," he says, and we laugh.

Keith—on my mind constantly: the sailboats in Palmer Cove, his steadiness. Light enters the kitchen, plays over "the furniture of the mind".

"You can smell the barrens on that jacket," I tell Alec, and he smells it. The green wool jacket I wore on that long canoe trip with Keith seven years ago.

"This wrapped around you in the barrens?" he asks.

"Than which nothing is more barren," laughing, worrying, again, about the loss of love.

"So explain to me what happened," Keith says in a dream.

* * *

Lescarbot wrote that he didn't come to see, he came to explore with his eyes. The process of love: following an image, watching it unfold. Objects, in this dying world, insist on speaking. Beaver used to talk, furs still do.

I smell Maria's apartment on my daughter's hair, the hours she has been away. She cried this morning when Alec left her there.

Fur is a carrier. It bears the smell of uneasiness, the taint of separation. Indians cut their hair in mourning, covered their dead with furs, protected them with soft warm darkness from the hard cold ground.

I stroke my daughter's hair as one strokes a fur coat, thinking about the animal.

Alexander Henry, a fur trader who travelled in Canada between 1760 and 1776, mentions a child who fell into a kettle of boiling maple syrup. While she lived her family made a continual feast to the Great Spirit to save and heal her. After she died they dug a grave and lined it with birchbark, laid the sweet scarred body of the child on the bark, placed alongside it an axe, a pair of snowshoes, a small kettle, several pairs of shoes, a string of beads, a carrying-belt and a paddle. The mother took a lock of hair from the girl's head, by which, she said, she would discover her in the afterworld.

The light goes and I turn on the lamp—soft talcum powder under an arm.

In the only surviving extracts from the *Account of the Captivity of William Henry in 1755 and of his residence among the Senneka Indians six years and seven months, until he made his escape from them,* William Henry writes about the Indian belief in an underworld "where there is only a kind of twilight. That in that country there are also the spirits of birds, beasts and fishes, and even of trees and plants. That all these spirits, a spirit can see and handle without hands."

An underworld where northern things have their afterlife: Sophie Football froze to death in a snowbank and was reborn as the light dusting of talcum powder under a child's arm.

Alec took our daughter for a walk and when he came back said, "She couldn't take her eyes off the snowbanks."

In 1793, a Northwest Coast Indian presented Alexander Mackenzie with a fur robe, and Mackenzie—in a foreshadowing of all that followed—gave a pair of scissors in return; Europeans snipped the lives of everything they encountered.

It was Mackenzie's custom to force Indians along the way to act as guides. One man, before accompanying him to the Arctic Ocean, cut off a lock of his hair, divided it into three parts, fastened one part to his wife's head and, uttering certain words, blew on it "with the utmost violence in his power. The other two he fastened with the same formalities, on the heads of his two children."

I wrap my fingers around my braid, smell thoughts on my fingertips . . . maybe, like hair, love grows again. In love patience can be so important.

Real Snow

In the small Connecticut museum the smell of musty books is as strong as the heat outside. Hannah's things are in a blue cardboard box, loose and in no particular order.

She has a beautiful hand. I find some of her letters, an account book with a few entries, a sample of her tatting, a photograph of Punney in an elaborate tasselled chair.

Hannah in the same chair—her hair in braided loops, a small flowered bonnet on her head, and those intelligent eyes looking out.

Joseph in the same chair, looking vague.

Browned envelopes addressed to "Esquimaux Joe and Hannah". Clippings from the *Groton Standard*. "They toured Great Britain attracting great crowds . . . in the hot crowded rooms Hannah caught cold and Johnny contracted pneumonia."

I keep looking for the diary. I ask, and to my enormous disappointment it turns out to be the nearly empty account book.

> *Punnia 3 Dollars.*
> *Hannah 4 Dollars.*
> *punna boots 2 Dollar 70 Cents*
> *8 socks 1 D. 20*
> *July 23 1873—Old Man give me 9 Dollars.*
> *From Joe 5 Dollars.*

She left so little evidence behind, unlike the men whose fate she helped discover. The members of the Franklin Expedition dragged boats behind them as they stumbled overland into cannibalism and death. They left behind a kid glove, a copy of *The Vicar of Wakefield*, a grass-weave cigar case, a pair of blue sunglasses in a tin case, a pair of calf-lined bedroom slippers, blue and white delftware teacups, a six-pence, dated 1831.

On Route 12 outside Groton, Connecticut the Starr Cemetery lies under a blazing sun. ("Hot not hurt me now," she wrote in one of her letters.) Circles of green lichen cover the tombstone.

> *Joseph Eberbing* [sic]
> *Hannah, His Wife, Died Dec. 31, 1876*
> *Aged 38 years.*

I look for Johnny's grave and can't find it. Nearby, a small weathered tablet, some of its words illegible, indicates where Punney was buried.

> *PUNNA*
> *adopted daughter*
> *HANNAH (INNUITS)*
> *Born Igloolik, July 1866*
> *Survivor of the Polaris*
> > *arctic Canada*
> *Chas. Francis Hall*
> > *with nineteen others*
> *ice floe, April 30*
> *adrift on the*
> > *of 190 days*
> *over 1200 miles*

Born as Tookoolito, buried as Hannah, she learned English, dined with Queen Victoria, shook hands with Ulysses Grant. Survived nearly seven months on an ice floe only to die three years later in Groton at the age of thirty-eight.

There was the child who died in New York. Another in the Arctic. The last in Groton.

The lecture tour through New England.

And that image of her final days—alone, surrounded by furs, sewing for the women of Connecticut.

They brought Hannah's hair down from the third floor, a black braid looped around in a small box with a note attached: "Hannah Ebierbing's hair. She was an Eskimo interpretor for Charles Hall's Arctic Expedition."

When the curator stepped out I lifted the cellophane off the small white box and touched the braid—like dry grass (against my sandalled feet in the cemetery), a bit coarse and all the oil gone. Pure black, 110 years old. An odd way to stroke someone's head.

I imagined the shape of her life—the first meeting with a white man when she was twelve and dressed in fur. The next meeting when she was fifteen and so curious and clever that she caught the attention of a merchant, Mr. Bolby. He invited her and Joe to come back with him to England, where they stayed two years, toured England and Scotland in native costume, dined with Queen Victoria in Buckingham Palace, officially got married. When they returned to Baffin Island Hannah brought dresses, hats, knitting needles, tea.

And then the next meeting, the most important one of all. "I heard a soft, sweet voice say, 'Good morning, sir.' The tone in which it was spoken—musical, lively, and varied— instantly told me that a lady of refinement was there greeting me. I was astonished. . . ." She stood in the doorway of Charles Hall's cabin on board a whaler, dressed incredibly in "a crinoline, heavy flounces, an attenuated toga, and an immensely expanded 'kiss-me-quick' bonnet."

A few days later he returned the visit. They sat in her

igloo, she brewed tea over an oil lamp and they shared the same cup because she had only one.

Hall was the key influence in her life, the one who took her south, "employed" her as translator, loved her, he said, as a daughter. An American eccentric, a mystical dreamer who rhapsodized about God and fell in love with the north, he had thrown over his life as an engraver in Cincinnati (daughter and pregnant wife) and begun to train for the Arctic in the late 1850s. He met Hannah in 1860 and spent the next two years living and travelling with her and Joe.

Seeing a white circle of frostbite on his face, she instantly applied her warm hand. Sensing how cold he was in the igloo, she took his frozen feet and pressed them against her naked side. When he set off on an expedition and failed to return, she climbed a hill day after day to look for him. And when he finally got back, "She gave me one look, and then the face I beheld was buried in hands trembling with excitement."

Hannah remained loyal to Hall until he died his bizarre death ten years later.

Flipping pages in the middle of the night—"a kind of hopeless anguish in the measured breathing of the wild creatures"—I think again of the movie *Bye Bye Brazil*, in which a small and dusty troupe of circus performers wanders the back roads of Brazil. Under a tent, a magician makes it snow on hot, delighted, upturned faces.

Hannah's face. Wide, strong features; neat hair pulled back; throat with its tidy collar and brooch; arresting eyes. Hannah was real snow. "In hot furs in hot rooms" she was the memory of it falling and the loneliness of its melting.

In 1862, in a sad migration, Hannah, Joe and the baby, Johnny, went south with Hall. He looked after them, put them on exhibit at Barnum's Museum in New York for a week. They were so popular they stayed two. They spent another two weeks on view at Cotting and Guay's Aquarial Gardens in Boston. And they travelled on his lecture tour to Providence, New Haven, Norwich, Hartford, Hudson, Elmira.

Lecture on Life Among the Esquimaux, by C.F. Hall Esq., lately returned from his Explorations in the ICY NORTH, bringing with him specimens of the Native Tribes, and their Dogs. The Esquimau Family Consists of E-BIER-BING (MAN), TUK-OO-LI-TO (WOMAN), TUK-ER-LIK-E-TA (CHILD) dressed in full NATIVE COSTUME, attended by their FAITH- FUL DOG, BAR-BE-KARK, and exhibiting some of their Hunting Implements.

Usually, partway through his lecture, Hall brought them out to gasps from the audience, who plied them with questions while they stood on stage with fish spears, dog harnesses, bows and arrows. Hannah was a favourite: her soft voice, her good English. *The New York Herald* claimed they "created quite a sensation".

Five months later they were ill, the baby seriously so. Another month and Hall was writing, "The loss was great to both of them, but to the mother it was a terrible blow. For several days after its death she was unconscious, and for a part of the time delirious. When she began to recover from this state she expressed a longing desire to die, and be with her lost Tuk-er-lik-e-ta."

The baby had died in New York at the age of eighteen months.

Only a few clues appear in the smeared, crossed out, tortured yet beautiful handwriting: she spent the first summer in the United States looking for cool breezes, she had tremendous affection for Sarah Budington—the whaling captain's wife who nursed them when they were sick—she brooded for years about Johnny's death, and, at least during her first stay in the south, she wanted to go home. "I wish this. Come home again this winter sometime."

Her words wander over the page. "I some time down Hearted and worry, and worry, poor my little Johnny I lost. . . . I like to have you take care my Johnny things till I come back. I know you do and no use cry. And cry mother than little Johnny. Cry an cry."

Some weeks after Johnny's death, Hannah "collected all his playthings and put them upon his grave. Visiting the spot some time after, she found that one article, a gaily painted little tin pail, had been taken away, and her grief was severe at the discovery."

Moved by their unhappiness, Sidney Budington, the whaling captain, offered to take them home on his next voyage. When Hall found out, he was enraged. "I trust neither I nor the Esquimaux will ever trouble your house again." *His* Eskimos, after all.

He moved them into his furnished rooms in New York, and from there Hannah wrote to Sarah Budington. "I been very hard time live New York . . . no like black eyes dark face and fat face. All time sick. Two winter I live New York sick. I no like this city."

In the spring of 1864, finally tired of his efforts to raise money for a more elaborate expedition, Hall booked passage for himself and the Inuit on a whaler. Before leaving he spoke to the Long Island Historical Society. Dressed in sealskins, Hannah and Joe sat behind him.

I'm struck by how neat Hannah's writing is sometimes, how crazily it veers over the page other times. She must have been writing when sick, or unsupervised—or sad.

"So good to me, so good to John, I think you, I loves my little John, I think him very much, some time you two. I never forget you. Thank you all things. Hannah." She signs her name variously Hannah, Hannah-li-to, Too-koo-li-to.

On July 16th, 1864 her writing is different again—blown across the page with huge gaps in the middle, and signed Tookoolito. She is back in the north.

When they returned it was not to their own people around Frobisher Bay but to Hall's destination hundreds of miles distant, at the northern end of Hudson Bay. Making his headquarters near Wager Bay and almost always accompanied by Joe and Hannah, Hall spent the next five years in arduous and unsuccessful attempts to find survivors of the Franklin Expedition. In 1865 Hannah gave birth a second time. Hall named the child King William after the island they were trying to reach.

King William's life was even shorter than Johnny's. At seven months he fell ill. Hall tried his medicines and they had no effect. One of the party then assumed the role of shaman and pointedly instructed Hannah to stop using white man's medicines, and to adhere to all taboos.

As Hannah watched her child die, Hall pressed his medicines upon her, the shaman his cures. The baby got weaker and weaker. Desperate to save him, she finally tried an old Inuit remedy for a very sick child and gave him away to another couple. He died on May 13th, eight months old. For an hour Hannah carried him in her arms before finally being persuaded to give him up.

In 1865, the first flowers were seen on June 16th. Purple saxifrage. That summer—the summer she was pregnant with King William—Hannah had pneumonia, and "raised blood direct from her lungs."

Joe smelled snow. He cut through it with a knife, "repeatedly smelling the snow until he satisfied himself that the seal had been there within a short time." He scraped down to the icy crust over the breathing hole, made a cut and waited. On a piece of fur, so as not to make a sound, he sat for hours. Waiting in silence on silence for a "softly-breathing noise beneath the snow."

When King William died, Hannah dressed him in a suit made of young caribou fur, wrapped him in a caribou blanket tied with thongs, "having a loop in it to go over the neck of the mother, who must carry the corpse," and climbed to the burial spot on a hill. She wouldn't wear her double jacket to protect herself from the storm, though "she had already borne for some days the inconvenience of wet feet; neither could her wet stockings be dried, nor the rips in her boots repaired . . . for one year her husband and herself must be very careful what they should eat, and that the same be not raw."

Earlier, the natives of Pelly Bay had given her two pairs of scissors, a cap-box, and some shot that came from Ross's *Victory*, done up in the skin of a deer's heart. Omens of her little one's death, and her own broken heart.

Hall was not without charm. He writes about combing the hair of a little Inuit girl, hair that had never been combed before. "She had but little that was long, the back part from behind her ears having been cut short off on account of severe pains in her head. How patiently she submitted . . . her hair was filled with moss, seal, and reindeer hairs, and many other things too numerous to call them all by name. Poor thing! Yet she was fat and beautiful."

It took an hour before he could draw the coarse end of a coarse comb through her hair.

"Her little fingers quickly braided a tag of hair on each side of her head. Then I gave her two brass rings (which is the fashion among the Eskimaux women) through which to draw the hair."

Hall's initial "uncontrollable joy" at being in the Arctic deteriorated after several winters into irritation and paranoia. In 1869 he returned south, taking Hannah, Joe, and Punney, the daughter they had adopted after King William's death. When Hall went north again it was for the last time.

In 1871 he embarked on his most ambitious and most doomed undertaking. Supplied with a crew and ship by the U.S. government, he set off for the North Pole—only to lose his life four months later. He fell suddenly and violently ill. Accusing his crew of having poisoned him, trusting no one but Hannah to prepare his food, he rallied briefly and then died.

He was buried on the morning of November 11th, 1871. Quiet, except for Hannah's sobbing.

The crew overwintered—fractious, unhappy, undecided about what to do. Ice prevented them from returning home that summer and they faced another winter in the same spot on the coast of Greenland.

On the night of October 12th, 1872, surrounded by icebergs and in the middle of a gale, the ship was "nipped" and thrown on its side. Some of the crew scrambled overboard while others threw down supplies. Hannah was on the ice hauling boxes away from the open water when the ice exploded and the ship broke free. Blown by the wind, it swung out to sea leaving Joe, Hannah, Punney and sixteen others stranded.

For seven months they drifted south. In his diary, *Wonderful Drift on the Ice-Floe*, George Tyson noted how alarmed Hannah and Joe were for their own safety—not because they were poorly clothed and nearly starving, but because of "the look out of the men's eyes". Joe redoubled his efforts to get seal.

On March 12th, as they approached warmer water, the floe shattered into hundreds of pieces. What remained was a chunk seventy-five by a hundred yards. Piling into a boat designed for at most eight people, they all made their way twenty miles to a larger piece of ice. On April 5th that piece shattered directly underneath them, splitting an igloo in two. So little ice remained that it was impossible to lie down. Again they took to the boat and found a larger floe.

"April 22nd. . . . Fearful thoughts go through my brain," wrote Tyson, "as I look at these eighteen souls, without a mouthful to eat. Meyers is actually starving. He cannot last long in this state. Joe has been off on the soft mushy ice a little way, but cannot see anything. We ate some dried skin this morning that had been tanned and saved for clothing, tough and difficult to sever with the teeth."

Washed over by waves, they huddled on each piece of ice until able to move to one slightly larger.

On April 30th, at five in the morning, a steamer spotted them through the Labrador fog. The crew of the sealer *Tigress*, out of Conception Bay, Newfoundland, "got out on our bit of ice and peeped curiously into the dirty pans we had used over our blubber fire. We had been making soup out of the blood and entrails of a last little seal. They soon saw enough to convince them that we were in sore need."

The survivors had drifted over 1,200 miles, the longest drift in history. A photograph taken in St. John's, Newfoundland, shows them in black suits and ties, Hannah in a black bonnet, all posed around their tiny boat against a backdrop of fake icicles. Two years later Punney was dead at the age of nine, her health broken by the long ordeal. The following year Hannah died from tuberculosis. Consumption, they called it; the body consumed the way ice is consumed.

After the ice-floe Hannah never went north again. All the survivors were taken back to the United States. They appeared before a government commission investigating Hall's death. When Hannah was questioned—she wept.

"Were you with him when he died?" she was asked.

"Capt. Budington called me in the morning; he said, 'Capt. Hall very near dying; most dead.' Then I got up and go see; his breath gone. (Joe and Hannah much affected). It was very hard at that time; our friend gone."

With Joe and Punney she moved into a farmhouse in Groton bought for them by Hall with money borrowed from a patron. Joe worked as a carpenter, and at sea. Punney went to school. Hannah sewed. One resident remembered her sitting on the floor chewing skins to soften them—feeling the north, and tasting it, but at a safe distance and with a full stomach.

Punney's death was the final blow. Writing to Sarah Budington, she said that Punney had been sick "34 todays", a description that captures the immediacy and eloquence of time running out.

The navy prepared an official account of the expedition. Its author, a Professor Nourse, wrote that only after finishing his report did he learn how strenuously Hannah and Joe objected to being called Eskimos. They were Inuit. Nourse attributed their aversion to a dislike of Greenland Eskimos; their racism, in other words, not his.

Hannah isn't even indexed. Tookoolito—see Ebierbing. And under Ebierbing—only Joe.

Yellowknife

Tongue-tied

When I was fifteen a little girl came around the corner of our house and said with great feeling, "I just *love* your big beaver teeth."

Twenty years later my daughter was teething and I was reading a book of beaver lore written in 1852. *The Castorologia* suggests putting beaver teeth around a teething child's neck to hasten the process. I grinned at her more often.

My fondness for beaver comes not just from the teeth but from the lost tongue. As an ancient race beaver were endowed with speech, then fell into mute disfavour. In my childhood I never stopped talking, they say.

This is Canadian being and becoming. Being at a loss for words, becoming embarrassed.

If I explored hesitation, would I find Cathay? A body of words, a captive soul, a small bound tongue?

Once I taped the sound of snow. I held a microphone between my teeth and taped myself skiing across a lake. The sound was gravelled over by the rubbing of my parka and the clicking of my teeth.

Now I keep writing feel for fell. Feel, fell, felt—a

new conjugation in the language of fur. I touched fur, and the memory is compressed and worn as felt, the texture of emotion, of felt things.

After my mother's father died, my mother had to sleep with her mother, from the age of seven until she left home at seventeen. All night long her mother ran her fingernails up and down the edge of the pillowcase, worrying about money, fretting the seams. That night-long scratching, a cloth record caught in a skip, robbed my mother of sleep and reproduced itself in me as a habit of thought—the bumpy, jerky rhythms of nervous hesitation.

Somehow it seems very Canadian. To be so in touch with self-doubt that its rhythms keep us awake.

A week ago I went to a party and bit the inside of my lip four times. Words twisted in my mouth and my teeth came down and clamped around their little bodies. Two holes, covered over by slowly healing white flesh, still throb where my teeth penetrated.

In 1649, fathers Brébeuf and Lalemant were trussed up with thongs of bark dipped in pitch and resin and set on fire. When Brébeuf continued to call upon the Iroquois to accept Christ, they cut off his lips.

So much for Canadian eloquence.

* * *

In Mexico I kept typing sad for said, and said for sad. Every conversation a lament.

"You feel bad," Alec told me, "and look for ways to feel worse."

Refusing, he was, to answer my question about love, posed just as we were about to fall asleep so that I would be sure to have a sleepless night, an excuse for anger, an opportunity for hate.

I dreamt that Alec and I were sitting in a restaurant and he was telling me about another woman pregnant by him, and how big her stomach was. Mine hadn't grown in a month.

Alec went to the gate with an umbrella. It was raining. *¿ No te mojaste?* he asked when he opened the gate. And I didn't understand.

"You didn't get wet?"

No—just covered with embarrassment. Not even able to say—simply, without apology—what do you mean?

In Mexico I knew a woman called Edit. Her name was pronounced ay-deet, and it was months before I awoke to her as an edit. She was small, as edits are, and she taped her life to Alec's, editing me out. They were the best of friends.

It must have been shame that blinded me to that particular word-play. I was envious of her volubility and liveliness, and aware of how petty my feelings were; I allowed only ay-deet to register. Besides, I liked her.

We talked about Alec. I said that probably I wasn't the best person for him. She outlined the kind of person he needed: someone who would lift him out of himself, who would come over when he was depressed and say, let's do this, let's do that. Someone flamboyant and upbeat. She seemed to be describing my opposite. Later, I realized she was describing herself.

At breakfast she licked honey off her fingers, then held them up, still sticky as she talked, too eager for conversation to walk away and wash them. Men buzzed around her. I came upon her once in the bathroom, standing on the toilet, naked except for her pants, which lay in a heap around her feet. Her boyfriend was taking pictures of her.

"Have you seen her eat candy?" a friend marvelled. "She can't get enough love."

When she broke up with the photographer, he went into a physical decline, and I teased her about it. "The light has gone out of his eyes. It must be because of you."

"No, no," she teased in return. "The point is that I'm so good for men, they feel so much more alive when they're with me, that when we break up nothing seems as vivid any more."

With Edit, the connection between the ability to talk well, to enjoy life and to love—came clear to me.

Standing in the January sun as it pours into the kitchen—so warm and white—I think of Margaret Avison, the name of one of her books of poetry: *Winter Sun*. I saw her speak once, and remember her gentle open enthusiasm when I went up to her at the end. She said, "You feel it too," and she asked my name. "I'll remember that," she said. Which was generous and uncynical and untrue.

"It's all right," Alec allows when I show him a poem of hers that I like very much. "What's a Manx cat?"

"From the Isle of Man," my eyebrows raised in surprise. "Off the coast of England."

"You know," he says, "I have an idea for your next project."

"What is it?"

"Colonialism. People who are colonized and don't even know it."

"Give me an example."

"Manx cat. The Brits are still there!"

Manx cat. All the hyphens in Avison's poetry echo the British poet Gerard Manley Hopkins. He too was religious and used hyphens to show connections not just between things but inside something, as in to-be-healed: that we will be healed and are made to-be-healed.

But a hyphen is also a break, a terse twist of small bones. A crowding together of words, lack of room to move, air to breathe: Avison locked in with her blind mother from six at night until eight in the morning, her hyphenated senses racing round and round in the divine shape traced by animals crazed with pain: perfect circles around a tethering stake.

Last night I had a conversation with Philip at the poetry reading. He was sitting down and I was standing so that I had a perfect view of his eyebrows which were inverted Vs, birds in flight. I stood so that I could escape, and so that he wouldn't feel trapped.

We talked about where we lived. He divides his time between New York and Amsterdam, where his wife lives. "I don't have an expatriate mentality," he said when I asked him which city he preferred. "New York."

He seemed interested as I talked about having lived in Mexico, wanting to live in Canada, living in the United States with a man who probably wouldn't like it. And where in Canada, anyway? Toronto? I've never had, I was going to say an affinity but couldn't remember whether it was affinity for or with, so said, I've never been that fond of Toronto. And Montreal, I'd have to learn a new language, which makes me feel old. As I rattled on in this fashion, it seemed to me he was interested, and so I sat down and his eyebrows became less alarming.

He talked about a Canadian friend who was always running Canada down until he did, and then his friend defended it. But to Americans, he said, Canada seems like a milquetoast version of the United States. I nodded. Yes, to most Americans, that's what it is.

There was talk all around us and the next part I didn't hear, and when I heard I didn't follow, so we got lost as I said,

Alec tells me I write about Canadian consciousness. He looked puzzled, what's that? I agreed, it is puzzling, and I'm not sure that's what I write about, but since Alec says it, there must be some truth to it: what it's like to be colonized, to live in such a climate. What it's like, I didn't say, to be considered milquetoast.

He talked about career ramifications, which was when I didn't follow at all, and then, does it affect you? he asked, your writing? And since I hadn't understood I just said no, it doesn't affect me at all because I'm so unpublished. Lost in conversation, not hearing, unheard, unpublished—a Canadian south of the border.

And then the little man with the big words said the next part of the reading would begin and I got up, victoriously, having talked till the end and not pitched into silence. As I went back to my seat Philip said, "I flew from Chicago to Toronto once and the difference was incredible. Toronto seemed so European."

"European?"

"Yes—clean—I tried to explain it to the cabdriver and he didn't understand at all."

Is clean European? I thought it was Canadian.

"It's the coffee," said Alec, lying awake beside me at midnight. We felt each other's restlessness.

"I'm hungry."

"So am I."

He went into the kitchen and came back with a nearly empty bottle of wine, a tin of sardines, a box of matzoh crackers. We picnicked on the bed.

"Galeano," he said, "talks about inventing a new language."

"You mean inventing words?"

"No, the way words are used."

And he gave Uruguay as an example. Under the dictatorship people referred to the government not as *la dictadura* but as *el proceso*.

"Imagine that," said Alec, "'the process'. People were so full of fear and self-deprecation, and the language reflected that."

"That sounds like me. Full of fear and self-deprecation."

"That's because you're from an underdeveloped country and won't admit it."

He looked at Phyllis Webb's picture on the back of her *Selected Poems*.

"She looks very Canadian."

"Why?"

"Don't get offended."

"I'm not offended—why does she look Canadian?"

"Something about the way she holds her head." He put his face, as she did, in the palm of his hand.

"Come on," I said. He laughed. "Come on, tell me. Why does she look Canadian?"

"Why are you so touchy?"

"I'm not touchy. Tell me."

He picked up the book and looked again. "It's. . . ."

"The control? She looks controlled?"

"Sort of—and the coat. She's wearing a coat with a high collar to keep off the north winds."

"What else?"

"She looks like she's from the prairies. The way she fixes her hair."

"Old-fashioned."

"That's the word. *That's* the word."

"You think I dress old-fashioned?"

"Well, yeah."

"Just because I wear hand-me-downs and never buy anything new."

"All right, you don't always look old-fashioned, but if you dressed up to get your picture taken you'd look like this."

"Straight. You're saying I'm straight."

"There's nothing wrong with straight."

"Bullshit. You hate straight."

He laughed.

"You think I'm straight."

"Why do you keep digging for compliments?"

Rabelais said Canada was so cold that words froze on people's lips and hung in mid-air till spring. In the fall sumac turns the colour of cut lips; we talk in a flushed monotone till snow falls.

Eloquence is an odd commodity. I say commodity rather than quality because the lack of it is something we carry around, a weight.

La Salle died trying to find a mouth. Having set off from Lachine, west of Montreal, he discovered the mouth of the Mississippi only to lose it when he returned by sea. He wandered along the coast of Texas through swamp and marsh until a handful of his starving men murdered him. They stripped his body and tossed it into the bushes.

From his map of Louisiana: The River Eure, the mouth of it Unknown. The River of Canoes, the Mouth of it Unknown. An Anonymous River, the Mouth of it Unknown. A beautiful River, being the first in the Nation of Cenis, the mouth of it Unknown. Tongue-tied geography.

In Toronto I met a furrier who learned how to sew fur by sewing newspapers. "They didn't want to waste any skins," he said. "It took me six months to start getting paid."

In 1870, during a stay in the Arctic, Charles Hall warmed his inkstand under furs. He used a small lamp to heat two metal plates which he alternated under his sheet of paper. The metal plate kept his fingers warm, dried the ink on the page, and kept the ink in his pen from freezing. Inside the igloo it was -42°.

Warming up words—rubbing them back to life.

Radio Friends

A magazine arrives—a picture of Sherry. Unseen for how many years? Seven. Since we worked together at a radio station in the north.

Hair cut close to the scalp. It must be the fashion. Posed. Well, we all pose. I look at the picture with a mixture of antagonism and regret.

"Is colonialism a question of loyalties?" I ask Alec.

"No, it's a question of who owns the country."

"But beyond that. Is it a question of who we're loyal to?"—thinking of Canadians loyal to Britain, others to the United States, but few loyal to each other. Few loyal to themselves.

And I suppose that's the point. Canadians expect to be dumped. We have the hurt, paranoid posture of the truly colonized, dumpee instead of dumper.

I remember pouring tea. This must have been ten years ago. Sherry stopped me when the cup was a third full. A third of a visit, I thought bitterly.

She sat with her back to the window, her face almost invisible in the waning light. I buttered a muffin, fingered the crumbs of our friendship.

"Things aren't the same as they used to be. I feel

dropped, sort of."

She smiled. "I knew we'd end up talking about this."

"You don't want to?"

"You're hot and cold," she said.

Surprised, "I don't think so."

"Sometimes you have all the time in the world to be friendly. Other times you barely look up."

"But I'm busy."

"I expect to be treated differently by you. I don't feel I can trust you, not with anything really important."

"Why?"

"You're unpredictable."

"Hot and cold."

"Yes."

What's the name for it when caribou mill around and patterns constantly change? Post-calving period, before they head in a surge south. But there's a name.

On the lake the ice turned black and candled. The surface melted into puddles which acted like dark lenses and melted the ice below into long sharp candle-like slivers.

In a dream I opened up my filing cabinet and everything in it had been replaced with Sherry's things.

When we listen to radio the words are clear. Anyone can understand. We listen to friends and never know exactly what they're saying. Or think we do in the warmth of the friendship, but in its cooling we don't know.

"Why do you wear makeup?" I asked Sherry.

"Why not?"

"Oh, I don't know. Not many people do any more."

"You should try it—instead of always putting down the way you look."

"I don't always put down the way I look."

"You should listen to yourself sometime."

She told me they'd be starting at seven and gave me half a sesame cookie to keep me going. We went into the studio and dramatized some children's stories for her radio program. My part was, "I'm down here." It took an hour and I said, "I'm down here," and crumpled an eggshell for a sound effect. I could have asked for a bigger part.

Peter told me that I sounded good on the radio but, if I wanted to be jealous, not as good as Sherry.

Jealousy is light gone bad, milk turning on the windowsill. I went off Sherry with jealousy. I turned, insecurity in the kitchen. And the stiff, unsure voice on the radio. Mine.

I listened to tapes to see how my voice compared with hers. I did it inconspicuously, guiltily, irresistibly. I wanted to know.

"Coffee?" she asked Ruth.

I watched them leave together. At the door she looked back, at my face, and laughed. "Coming?"

When I caught up with them she wore the same bright impatient look. I tried to make amends, tried to be light-hearted. I knew she was watching me and yes, when I glanced up, she was, but not with interest—assessment —as though she knew me thoroughly and was simply curious to see which side I would show, not that she would be surprised, ever.

We went up the street and slid into a booth at the back of the restaurant. My doughnut arrived first, with the coffee, but I let it sit there until she bit into her sandwich. Then I ate, brushing my fingers at the corners of my mouth and across my chin after each bite, afraid that the powdered sugar, afraid that a crumb, was clinging.

She talked about Jim and the documentary they were making. She was making with Jim, not with me. The interview they couldn't get (their shoulders touching, as they went over their list), she had tried one person and he just wouldn't talk. I said, when we did our program, and she said, yes, but this is different. Is it? I couldn't find that one guy and then we realized we could get around it. Can't you get around it?

"No. Jim and I [Jim and I] think we should just keep trying till we get the interview. He's got a contact who might help."

"Oh."

I pressed the crumbs together and licked them off my fingertip, traced circles on the plate.

"I have to get back," she said.

"Another five minutes," I said.

"I wish I could."

Interviewing helped with loneliness. I met new people and sat down with them and talked. At least it kept isolation away, that sea, but not this other, of salmon going upriver and Sherry wriggling her tail out of sight, all moving in one direction, away, as I tried to chart the emotion.

A white basin for washing, slow, quiet, disturbed in the mornings. The slightly controlled panic after waking.

The ice was green, the snow lavender. Smoke flapped out of chimneys. It had turned very cold.

I imagined a screen door. An open window, birds on the grass, and roses, white roses.

What did I notice? The bunch of letters in front of me, the number of times the letterbox was empty. The cracks in the pale blue wall, the iced-up windows, the stripes of ice on the inside of the pink front door. Even the inside doorknob was covered with ice.

Next to the window, I felt the presence of cold beyond the window, and the cooling effect it had on the air inside.

I went shopping and looked for the kinds of things she wore. I started to dress like her. I wore t-shirts, and a necklace. I registered each person who was attracted to her. I watched her slim body move through the office.

We were working late one night. She finished putting together the sound effects and went into master control and sat at the console. I remained at the tape recorder, my animosity welling up with such force it sickened me.

I couldn't stop imagining a story in which a jealous friend becomes privy to information, and reveals that information to hurt the friend.

I had known the first time I went to her apartment. One bedroom had a big double bed front and centre. The other bedroom, "Karen's room", was tiny with a single bed pushed up against the wall. And the way she used the word "we"—noticeable, different.

And yet I was surprised.

"Why didn't you tell me before?" I asked her.

"I don't know. I've told lots of people sooner. I guess I wasn't sure you were ready."

She hugged me as I was leaving, then leaned back, her arms still around me. She leaned forward and kissed me on the lips.

"Don't be afraid," she said. "I'm not going to rape you."

Her lips were very thin and soft. They felt oddly unresistant, spongy—fleshy and alive but not quite.

A few letters have arrived. I haven't answered them. One long letter came to Mexico. It assumed a friendship—a friendliness on my part—that flew in the face of fact. She seemed to think everything was simple when nothing was simple. That's something she didn't learn from her years in the north. Thawing, and a certain thawing has happened, isn't smooth.

Dead Air

Writing about dead air as snow falls, the visual equivalent. In that small radio station in Yellowknife, a poem pinned to the control room wall summoned up a car crash on the highway; from the still wreckage of bodies and metal a car radio kept blaring. Do you ever wonder, the poet asked the broadcaster, where your voice goes?

Our voices carried over snow, reading community announcements to Joe Punch in Trout Lake: pick up your C.O.D. parcel at the Fort Simpson post office. To the Chocolates in Fort Rae, and the Wandering Spirits.

To Emily Greyeyes, Alice Ottereyes, Helen Fishbone, Alizette Potfighter. "Debbie Lynn had a baby boy, six pounds, eight ounces, both doing well."

The intimacy of radio: talking to someone and talking, of course, to no one. Alone in the studio. Which must be why so many shy people work for radio.

"The mistakes don't matter," Tony, the tech, assured me. "It's the recovery that counts."

"Do I sound nervous on air?" I asked him.

"No," he said. "You sound like you're falling asleep."

Outside, old tape spilled over the garbage bin, blew

in dark tangled loops down the street, over the frozen lake, out into the arctic air—words on words, corrections on corrections, the tape reused until it was completely white with splicing tape, frostbitten with corrections, hard and numb.

"But your voice is too soft," they told me.

"Will you tell her not to whisper," a caller said.

Simultaneously contained in that glass womb, and exposed. That was the tension. To have the sensation of safety, and the underlying inescapable fear.

In Winnipeg I walked down Portage Avenue to a shop that sold love aids. What was in the window? Something red—a quilted heart? I walked upstairs and a very slim woman gave me speech lessons. She talked to us about the voice on the mask of the face. I remember a Chinese boy who couldn't make himself understood at all, and an actor.

"Red leather, yellow leather. . . . Leroy breeds really keen steeds. She freezes beef each spring."

In Winnipeg I got a permanent, but my voice stayed flat.

Squeaking. Then quiet. I began the script over again. A mouse? Again I stopped. I walked over to the wall, bent down and saw the trap under the table. The mouse lay on its side, not pinned, stuck. Some kind of glue? I leaned under the table, lifted the trap, and the mouse rippled.

I found a security guard. "There's a mouse," I said, "in a trap in the studio. It's still alive."

"They flush them down the toilet," he said.

We went back to the studio and bent down to look. He lifted the trap, and again grey heaved.

"Will it die—drown?"

"You want to set it free?"

"No."

"You want to set it free?"

"No," impatiently. How could it be let free, the lower half mutilated? "No, of course not—just killed."

He took the trap into the hall.

"I'm sorry," I called after him.

I had laid the script on the piano. I picked it up again. A large studio. I read the opening to the interview with Joan Sutherland. Had the mouse heard my voice? And squeaked?

Hers in trouble too. She had received admirers in her dressing room—in dark glasses, the huge face, red lips, dark grey (mouse grey) makeup on her cheeks where they tried to make her face appear narrower. She signed autographs, nodded, smiled—but couldn't talk, wouldn't talk, to protect her voice. It was hoarse.

And now my voice was reading about her voice. The other quiet.

"Are you obsessed about your voice?" I asked. Worried that it will change, go—squeak?

"Not at all," she said. "It's a gift. And if I'm sick—well, that's an occupational hazard."

The voice, she called it, which had a trapped sound too. She wanted to retire, Richard Bonynge didn't, and she was his drawing card.

"Shame on you," she protested when he said he wanted to go on indefinitely.

"They're honey and glue," the security guard told me. Immobilized down one side.

Ezra Pound went mad on air. All that eloquence went crazy. Dead air can go crazy too—in its quiet way. The dead air inside, the emptiness.

We appear by disappearing. Into shyness. Self-consciousness. Which we try to edit out. But in the process all that embarrassment simply spills onto the floor of the mind. Not erased, oddly alive. Stuck on one side, rippling on the other.

I still waited to stumble, and I did, into what? The electrifying silence which follows a mistake. I listened to all the fumbles I was going to make, and then I made them. I heard them conceived, I heard them born, I heard myself dying on air.

Auntie Muriel still used the term "listening to the wireless". Feeling it give way.

The summer I worked in Toronto I lived in a one-room apartment on Carlton and watched the red Ramada Inn sign out my window, one "A" and its "I" out. It was the summer of the constitutional debate, that long and rancorous struggle to "repatriate" the constitution. On Trudeau's behalf, Jean Chrétien travelled the country talking about bringing the constitution home.

I woke up in Ottawa in the Lord Elgin Hotel. The windows didn't open. Despite summer, the room was winter. I talked with oil men who hated Marc Lalonde, the perfectly bilingual energy minister. "He can't even speak the language," they said, inarticulate in two languages which is the English Canadian way.

I took the train a lot that summer, commuting on the weekends between Toronto and Windsor. I kept imagining train wheels crunching over a wrist, or lower arm. Or the lid of a trunk inadvertently being slammed on my arm, and opened, for my arm to slip out, broken.

At night I tried to fall asleep by thinking about Yellowknife. I imagined walking around Latham Island: rain, wind, sand on my fingers as I picked up a stick and threw it for Stan. But no good. Birds picked up outside. And the horror of light.

"We can dovetail," they said, swooping in on me, Ross and Tom, it must have been, the two of them dovetailing to "vet" my piece.

And where does that word come from? Veteran? Of editing wars? No—veterinarian. To examine or treat as a veterinarian does. The body of a documentary, tape mangled on the floor.

Around the table documentaries were assigned and tensions felt. Ellen's anger after they cancelled her interview. Her face, the set of her mouth, the whole table set with tension. Mine. Fear, such fear. And Randy, using a razor blade to cut his nails.

On the first of July we broke the meeting at noon to watch the governor general and Trudeau sing "O Canada." Ross said, "Canadians are so boring."

I had dinner with an English journalist who wore me down with his frustrations about Canada. "The dullness, lack of style, don't you see it?" he asked.

"Name a good Canadian writer," he said, "one with pizzazz and international esteem, one with influence. Name a journalist with style."

He felt crushed by the literalmindedness of Canadians. By the copy editor who had read his lead, "Terry Fox is 24 years younger and a hundred times fitter than the other Canadian hero, Ken Taylor," then turned to him and asked, "How do you know he's a hundred times fitter?" And changed it to "perhaps 100 times fitter."

Serenity: a Chinese woman selling flowers. I walked past her twice, two hours between, and both times she was in the same position—sideways to the pedestrians, arranging flowers in the cart as though not really selling. The second time she was wearing gloves. The first time her slim hands cupped the flowers, but as though not selling.

In the darkness of the plane a black woman held a

bouquet of yellow and white roses, short ones, wrapped in brown paper. Her wee daughter sat beside me, hair full of multicoloured barrettes. No fragrance but the colours alive in the dark, almost luminous, the child asleep and leaning against my arm.

More than overblown, they were wilted. Her head at such a bent angle.

We landed in Miami. Palm trees bent over in torrents of rain, my wet blouse, the surge of perfume—was it frangipani? Streets were green, lush, steaming. In the taxi I kept touching my face, the different texture, moist without being wet, wind through the open window. Unlike anything I had ever felt before.

In a backyard on Eleventh Avenue, yellow bell flowers covered the fence, and the smell of yellow rice and fried bananas filled the air. "What are the spices?" I asked. "Oregano and cumin," they said.

Come-in, their son pronounced it. Welcome.

I rented a car and drove outside Miami to the Krome detention centre. I drove bewildered by the traffic, bathed in sweat, to interview refugees who had fled Cuba and now wanted to return. "There is no love here," one of them said, pronouncing it l-ah-ve, a commodity I had never heard of, it seemed, in the way he meant.

The air held us. I interviewed people and they pressed up against me. Amid all the old tension, the old fear of working, was this new sensation, of new air—as though in that hot climate I had shed my skin, and walked now hand in glove, my hand in a soft glove.

Back in Toronto my thoughts stayed steadily on Miami as the air changed and became fall. I cracked open a hard-boiled egg and the white reminded me of stucco walls. I left two peaches on the table beside my bed and smelled them upon waking. Peeled one, and discovered that moist air again—dewy, soft.

In the greenhouse in Allan Gardens I found the yellow bell flowers: Golden Trumpet, *Allamanda Cathartica*. Emptied, yes, for a moment, emptied of tension.

New York

Nara

I taste cold milk and the whole barrens rise up. Warm milk— and the tropics: heavy and overripe against the lovely cold taste of nothing on the landscape.

We've emptied our apartment in Salem.

In New York we stay with a fur seamstress. Nara left Cuba in 1960 and spent the next twenty-five years sewing mink coats in Manhattan. From one warm climate to another.

I hear crickets at five in the morning, roosters in the distance, but not far. Nara lives in a house beside the railway tracks. Trains go by thirty feet away, and passengers wonder —I always did—who lives in places like this.

Nara makes strong sweet coffee in tiny cups which she brings to us with unfailing courtesy every morning and afternoon. "I come home thinking of coffee," and she lifts off the lid so I can smell it.

In the bathroom, bottles of lotion, perfume, makeup fill every shelf. A long black hair clings to the bathtub. Caribou with their heavy black female eyes vanish into trees and leave hairs on the rim of the river.

We carry ideas from one place to the next and use them to orient ourselves: the density of New York versus the density of snow. Nara hurt herself shovelling the sidewalk, and now her back remembers snow all year round.

Yesterday my daughter saw snow. She crawled through the Eskimo exhibit in the Museum of Natural History, pulling herself up on the wooden railing that runs alongside a window of snow implements—probes, knives, goggles, shoes, sticks. In her green sweater she was the only leaf, shifting along, unsteady on her feet.

We saw caribou, "large spreading hoofs suited for travel over the soft muskeg and deep snow . . . a life of continuous travel."

We saw mink. Active at night, the description said. As was Nara, sewing them.

"Say snow," I say to my daughter.
"Knows."
"Snow."
"Knows."

A nose for snow. At five in the morning (pitch-black because I've been sitting in the dark drinking coffee) Alec drops her in my lap. Her hand snakes out behind her and feels its way with uncanny precision to my powdered doughnut. She pulls it towards her, manoeuvres it to her mouth, tucks it in—all without looking.

"This is pony. They say it's mink, but it's pony," and Nara shows me one of the coats she has made.

In 1670, Jasper Danckaerts explored Manhattan and "sometimes encountered such a sweet smell in the air that we stood still, because we did not know what it was we were meeting." All the perfumes and furs in Manhattan: flowers without stems, animals without trees.

To be writing about fur again—the connecting thread, the hair in my soupy geography. Draw a line from Yellowknife to Winnipeg, over to Toronto, down to Mexico City, back up to Salem, and over to New York and you'll see the hairline crack of my particular coming apart and staying together.

My daughter is asleep, so is Alec. I'm at the kitchen table listening to crickets. Thinking about fur—other endings.

Brooklyn Suite

Yellow is the colour of the last leaves to fall. The last colour a blind person sees. The world losing its sight.

I followed Alec in the yellow rent-a-truck as it scudded down the highway into the blindness of New York. We parked on a block without a single tree and walked up two flights of stairs to our new apartment. Bright/dark/dim: the movement of light—a kitchen with a southern exposure, a middle room with no windows at all, a living room with a sort of twilight.

We'll set up the grow-light, I said. Unused since Yellowknife.

* * *

Dark middle—movement of our days. Holding, rocking, worrying, not much else. Crying when my daughter throws up her medicine.

The middle room is cooler and we keep her there. I read Phyllis Webb's *Naked Poems*, stroke my daughter's little body on the bed. So much white on the page.

Clothes blow into each other's yards. We meet over a towel, a shirt, a dropped sock. Is it yours?

The power of empty clothes. My daughter's, Aunt Sarah's, which I wear. (Aunt Sarah died a month ago.) I iron my daughter's shirt. Her body irons itself.

An old Matisse calendar hangs on the kitchen wall. Like sickness, calendars suspend time. From 1983, paper cutouts of wild poppies. Matisse made them in bed after he was too old and sick to paint. Our daughter snips our lives to fit her own.

* * *

In the living room a white skull oversees the twilight. Six inches of snow have fallen. In the windows the childguards are layered up with snow. When I hear my daughter crying and she isn't crying, what am I hearing?

Wind rushes through sway-backed windows, the hanging plant turns. Small disturbances—from all of yesterday's visitors. The uneasiness of having a quiet party with too many people and too many pauses. Music, but too late.

Then out of the blue, "They found his body with his beard shaved and his hands cut off." Debbie. Argentina.

Rasmussen told a story about strange sounds hovering in the air, "like the ghost of words; as if one were trying to speak without a voice." They searched, found a snow shelter and, inside, a woman seated on the floor, almost naked, having eaten most of her own clothing. She whispered, "I am one who can no longer live among humankind, for I have eaten my own kin."

Blood trickled from the corners of her eyes, "so greatly had she wept."

In the living room I look more closely at the skull mask, and stop still. The eye sockets are red.

Saturday morning light . . . which I increase with an almond croissant, stopping at 40th Street on my way to 42nd. Early December.

Bare branches are soft mirrors which glisten, enticing ravens to approach (a saxophone squawks on the curb). Yellowknife again.

Coat open, fingers hopping on a cold fence, Raven pleads for silver moons, copper suns which we throw into his case. He closes it, and night falls.

Yellowknife. The design butter leaves on a knife. Patterns of light in a raven's beak.

Pine needles impregnate us, as do these needles of light our eyes, with relief—cool air descends from the north and plays on the steps of the New York Public Library.

Inside, at a long table under a blue lamp, I read about Chapewee, the first man, who found among the stars "a fine plain and a beaten road", and on the road set a snare made of his sister's hair. It caught the sun as do fine hair-like twigs outside.

December is the radiance of reduced light. My daughter takes hold of my face with her little hands, the same hands that stroke my arm as she sucks. The fever is gone.

* * *

I lean out the window to cool off. Lovely breeze at nine in the morning, fire escape on my right—thinking of summer, escaping the heat as Django barely did. His blackened fingers after the fire.

I put him on again, playing with Stephane Grappelli (cafés, leaves, light), yellow light on the fire escape, mangoes in children's mouths. On a bus in Mexico they pulled them in and out of their mouths—yellow tongues, peeled tongues, sensual and mute.

My daughter's blonde hair is the last colour I want to see.

David

The mail arrives with a letter from David. A barely readable
envelope, and inside, a card with nothing on it, a handful of
stamps, a smaller envelope with my daughter's name written
on it and Brooklin, misspelled, and New York—petering out.

A photograph he took hangs above my desk. One of
a series shot in Yellowknife of weeds in water, weeds in
snow. This one is weeds in snow. The stems stick up like
fine, precise calligraphy: stick legs, his legs, now.

Last spring he was very thin. He still limped but no
longer needed a cane. The leg infection that "went crazy".

"Why?" I asked.

A pause. And then, "I might as well tell you."

Our conversation was on the phone. We agreed to
meet the next day. I toyed with the idea of leaving my
daughter behind, but it would have hurt him so much. And
how could she have come to any harm?

"The hardest thing," he said, "is to have so little
energy."

In the kitchen he washed his hands carefully. "They
say that's important. Not to let any dirt get under your nails."
He called at 1:55 a.m. Alec answered. When he crawled
back into bed I asked him what David had said.

"It's all roses and hospitals here, so tell Lizzie to send

me a rose. A rose is a rose is a rose. Send it to the children's hospital, yeah, the children's hospital. Or send it to a hospital there and I'll get it quicker."

"What else did he say?"

"He said he was walking with a cane and a rich couple in fur passed him, and he thought of you. I asked him how his mother was and he said, fine—worried about me, I'm worried about me, I'm worried about my friends. They all think I'm dead. But I'm not dead. Then he switched to French. He said, I'm here in Toronto. No. I'm in Mexico. No, I'm in France. In Toronto. No. Mexico. I'm in Mexico. I bought a ticket. I'm going at Easter."

"He was so brilliant," his mother said when we went to visit, and she burst into tears. "That's what's so hard. To see him now."

She hurried away so that he wouldn't see her crying.

Her insomnia keeps step with his. When he can't sleep he wanders around and changes everything in the house, writes on things, paints on them, cuts them up and pastes them to other things. And so she stays awake too. A month without sleep. Bringing us tea.

David said, "When I start to quarrel with my mother, the answer is to go from one room into another."

In his bedroom pictures of us were on the wall: bathing our feet in the stream at Palenque, buying tortillas, climbing a ruin. Next to the pictures were several Mexican masks, a photograph of our hotel in San Cristóbal, a Mennonite quilt, a child's drawing of a bone.

David sat down in a rocking-chair and reached for a book about the artist Joseph Beuys. He showed us two photographs of Beuys with a cane. "And my brother just happened to give me this the other day." A hat, almost exactly like Beuys' fedora. David put it on.

"It's almost too much," he said.

Then he put buttons, embroidery thread, pieces of scrap Christmas paper in a box already full of things he had saved for us. He threw in a handful of change. "Do something with them," he said.

We were leaving—David was lying down upstairs, we had said goodbye and were already in the driveway—when his mother hurried out and from the porch said to us in a low voice, "The painting. You should take it back."

One of my mother's paintings. David had asked to have it—a portrait of a bandaged torso. "I think it would heal me."

Now his mother was anxiously bringing it back out. "I'm afraid he'll draw all over it," she said.

I smelled Mexico so clearly a little while ago. Cuernavaca. The smell of the street where I first stayed. A dream from last night?

When David came to see us we took him to Chiapas. In the square in San Cristóbal a woman sat on a bench with a wide bucket of meringue at her feet. Soft, white, shiny, sweet. In the morning David's breath was visible in the air when he leaned out the window.

David and I walked to Zinacantán. Coming down the hillside he picked a pink thread off a bush and put it into his notebook. I noticed him noticing, which was how I noticed for a long time. We walked into the full colour of the village: the lipstick pink of tunics and shawls, the lighter pink of peach blossoms. Threads and petals were underfoot.

Pink knocked on pink: two girls at a door.

Pink stretched out on the grass: two men.

Pink stretched out on the floor: Maria's weaving. Was she working on it when we knocked?

We asked if she could make us something to eat,

there was no restaurant in the village. Only tortillas and salt, she answered. Eggs? Yes, she could make eggs. She sent her younger brother off to buy them while we waited inside the little house.

Her eyes were bad, she told us. She was eighteen.

"Would glasses help?"

"We don't wear glasses."

"Why?"

"We don't."

"Custom?"

"Yes," she said.

Later she showed us wedding pictures of her older sister, and her brother. He wore glasses.

We sat on the only two chairs, David and I, with a low narrow table between us. Maria brought sweet coffee, and questions. Is it colder in Canada than here? How do they make houses? What do they eat? Can you live on wheat? Here, she said, people are strong eating corn, and they say that in Europe and North America people grow fat on bread.

"Are you married?" she asked. We smiled, no.

And then, "How old are you?"

"Guess David's age," I said.

"Fifty," she said.

I laughed but David was shocked. At the time I thought it was vanity, and it surprised me.

David was reading a book set in Mexico in 1932. An Indian died and his family put tortillas in his coffin. They wet his lips several times for the long journey.

Outside Chamula we walked through the cemetery on the hill. I jotted down all the different spellings for died: *fallecio, fallesio, fahecio, failecio, facio.* Small crosses were painted black, or white and blue, the lettering was crude.

For over a year David had already had deep and

vicious boils that wouldn't go away. The leg infections that eventually "went crazy".

One afternoon while he slept outside in a hammock, Alec and I made love in the tent and conceived our daughter. I've always thought of David as her guardian angel. Death? As a guardian angel?

* * *

A valentine from David. I open the envelope and hearts fall out, keep falling out. Ten of them cut from fluorescent orange and pink paper, from regular red and white paper, and from a snapshot. Cut rather crudely. They make my eyes swim.

In fact, only nine. The tenth is the torn corner of the red envelope.

Also a poem.

> *My heart broken*
> *By my cane*
> *Let's you and I talk about Matisse.*

We were driving through snow listening to jazz. In a warm car, warmed by jazz, listening to snow. And now I'm in a hot bath and Coleman Hawkins continues in the other room. Thirty-two hours of him on the radio.

Eskimos listened to jazz in the twenties. Rasmussen came upon an igloo where they were starving, and fed them. Then he watched as they produced a gramophone and told him "in sober earnest" that jazz was as soothing to a full stomach as it was comforting to an empty one.

Hot music in a snow house.

Matisse—in my house. Cards from his series called Jazz decorate the walls; the full colours of hunger satisfied. I send one to David.

In the months when David suspected he had AIDS but before he knew for sure, he made a series of drawings using black ivory pigment made from burned bones. He set up a tent in his studio, laid pieces of paper inside, used a bellows to blow in the pigment, and allowed it to settle on the paper. He drew on the dust with his fingers. He said he wanted the drawings to resemble the marks left in snow on a tranquil day.

A few years ago we walked over to Broadview and Gerrard and went into three Chinese groceries. We looked at bowls and talked about ways of containing loneliness. David said it would be a struggle not to become isolated, I would have to fight. He advised me to fill my days as full as possible by having friends over and by going to visit.

He reached for a can of lichees. "You've eaten them?"

"No."

"Well," he said, "we'll have to eat them in these green bowls," reaching for two, "because the colour of the lichees against this green is beautiful."

We made our purchases and walked to his apartment, where he opened the can of lichees, washed the two bowls, spooned in the fruit. The lichees were white against the green. I told him why Keith and I had separated. He was surprised, and not surprised.

His apartment was orderly in a sensual way. In the kitchen a wooden shelf ran along the counter just above the sink. On the shelf sat other Chinese bowls, and above them— a photograph of clay pots arranged against a wall in Pompeii; the bowls echoed the pots in the photograph.

In the hallway I looked at his photograph of an old house in Quebec. He pointed out the precise use of white: the lacy woodwork on the double screen doors was white, but the doors had been left a weathered grey; the posts at the side of the steps were white, but the steps and the verandah were grey. The effect was considered, restful.

Luxurious, like cream. David said he needed cream for the sauce he planned to make. We walked to a store and he asked me to get the cream while he ordered the meat at the counter. I was slow, comparing prices. When I reached for the 18 percent, David was already beside me taking the 35 percent. He smiled, "Why not?" So we had the richest of sauces.

As we ate I looked at the reflections in the window beside us: the lamp hanging low over the middle of the table, the bottle of wine, our profiles. The wind blew and the branch of a scotch pine brushed against the window. We were four floors up. David had chosen the three most beautiful discarded Christmas trees on his block, carried them home, wrapped a rope around the trunks, and hoisted each one up to his apartment balcony. He built three bases for them, and set them upright alongside his window.

Some time after my marriage with Keith ended, David said to me, "I've been thinking a lot about colour. It's so intimate. Like you and the rubrum lilies."

"You mean the wedding bouquet?"

"Yes. We cut them and arranged them and handled them. It's very intimate."

We had done this the night before the wedding. I had cut the flowers in the garden and taken them over to David's apartment, where he made them into a bouquet.

"The colour," he said, "with your dress. I remember your dress being mostly grey, and the colour of the lilies set it off."

We cut the stems and held the flowers this way and that, our hands touching, till we settled on the final arrangement.

David continued to talk about flowers—he had bought

five sprigs of freesia and we smelled them over dinner—and that was intimate too. Next to each other, conversing, next to the flowers.

"He's not here," his mother says when I call. "He's in Toronto and he's in a lot of trouble. Last night he demolished Stephen's apartment, and tonight he's supposed to stay with Eric—I don't know whether you know him—and he hasn't got any money because he lost his wallet."

"What do you mean, demolished?"

"Well, he demolished a lot of things around here too. He paints on everything, spills paint everywhere—because," she says, "he just wants to paint."

Stephen said months ago that he couldn't deal with David any more. He said that one night David had talked nonstop without taking a breath for seven hours. All of it nonsense. Brain damage. Memory loss. Unable to tell the time. Unable to count. Therefore unable to take his own medicine.

He would get up in the middle of the night and frantically write notes to himself, none of them legible. Demand to be waited on hand and foot. Insist—for four hours—that the colour television was no good and they had to buy another.

One night Stephen called friends over to help because he couldn't "settle him down", and "as soon as they stepped in the door he was as good as gold." The minute they left, "he was pounding on my door again and I knew I'd be up with him till four in the morning."

Stephen put David on a bus to Owen Sound. He called David's parents to tell them he was coming, and they pleaded with him to wait a day until they could come and get him. Stephen put him on the bus anyway. David—not knowing where he was—got back off, wandered around, soiled himself, finally got hold of a friend by phone, who came and picked him up.

After David "demolished" his apartment—upsetting drawers in his desk, pulling books off shelves—Stephen had the lock to the apartment changed. This was the apartment he and David had shared for seven years.

David can still write postcards and short letters, though after writing one his hands are very tired.

"What do they feel like?"

"A thousand pins and needles."

He says he can't move "except with a cane and a wall". Sleep is very difficult because his legs go into painful spasms—they're always jumping—and that wakes him up.

Stephen is bedridden, he tells me. And his mouth and throat are so full of thrush that he can't talk. "Or so his mother says."

"You don't believe her?"

"I don't know. She's cut him off from everybody."

"You think she's trying to keep you from talking to him?"

"Or maybe it's just Stephen. He's cut himself off. He'd be one to do that. And you know, I love him, but I'm ready to move on. And you know what I'm ready to move on to?"

"What?"

"A relationship with a lady. I already have someone in mind—but she's not available."

I go through the box of things David saved for us: a picture of a hummingbird torn from a magazine, buttons, a small tourist pamphlet of a church in Alsace, clump after clump of embroidery thread, a scrap of tie-dyed material, fuchsia and white, two knitting needles, a piece of lace, a package of hooks and eyes, a notebook written in backwards and upside down. The only words I can make out are To Stephen, and Nose Knows. Colour samples for paint: tangerine, vienna blue, peacock green. A postcard addressed to Sochi Elizabeth Jean Hay. More lace, two whistles, a pink balloon, shoelaces, a stamp from Cuba, one from Vietnam, one from Laos.

He calls to tell me that Stephen has died. "Me next," he says.

"What did David say?" Alec asks.

"Just that Stephen died yesterday, and me next."

The distance on the telephone—seven hundred miles—and the distance of my reaction, I know. David's quiet voice.

"He isn't able to go upstairs any more," I say. "He's confined to the first floor now. His feet won't move."

More samples: Van Gogh yellow, garnet red, pink casino, billiard green, firmament.

A crochet needle.

"Make use of them," David kept saying. "Do something with them."

I write to Stephen's mother. In addressing the envelope I put down, unthinkingly, Stephen—then white it out.

When David was small he took the dry turds out of his diaper and lined them up in a perfect row on the windowsill. As a young man he made a series of drawings by puncturing large sheets of paper with a sewing machine. In other drawings he scored lines with the blade of a meat cleaver. In some there were barnacle-like holes.

"Bullets," he said.

At the Scarborough shooting range he pinned sheets of paper on the wall and two policemen shot holes in them.

They used .38 calibre pistols in order to make pencil-sized holes.

"Were they interested?" I asked. "Curious?"

"No, the only thing one of them said was, 'Let's try a shotgun.' "

The drawings were so peaceful and intimate. How can this be?

Down the street in a friend's studio three photographs hang on the wall. They show a dead dog lying in a woods, the fur dusted with snow, then covered lightly as though with wax, then covered completely. A burned down candle—soft, splayed out—a puddle with just a bit of height. Softly burning snow, snow softly burning in a dead dog candle.

The dog must have been hit by a car, and dragged itself into the woods to die.

I reread a letter from David.

Dearest Liz,

The garden out the window is exquisite, we've been getting rain. Early morning light makes it so beautiful. The cat is lying on the deck washing himself.

The Aids disease now has me crippled up to my waist plus my hands are partially useless. Still try and draw a little but it's next to impossible. Cat fell asleep. Sunshine.

Raspberries have been abundantly ripe in my sister's garden. [He draws a raspberry and shades it red.]

The hibiscus on my desk is in bloom. Exquisite colour—coral.

David Thompson

At the New York Public Library I untie the string around a book, take off the protective envelope, open the pages. Bits of brittle paper fall onto the table like confetti.

In 1810 Thompson journeyed into snow. He went up the Athabasca River and across the Rockies into mild Pacific air which only deepened and softened the snow so that he could barely move. On January 10th some of his men used a twenty-foot pole to probe for the bottom. They found "a beautiful blue; the surface was of a very light colour, but as it descended the colour became more deep, and at the lowest point was of a blue almost black."

Five of his men deserted. "Everything was so novel, so very different from what they had been accustomed to see, the trees of immense size, the great depth of snow they were sure would never thaw, their hearts failed them. . . ."

Thompson and the remaining three dug a hole ten feet square in the snow, lined it with cedar boards and lived there for three months. In April they set off down the Columbia River in a canoe made of cedar boards hewn from the surrounding forest and sewn together with fine roots of pine. The fragrance. To travel in one's own handiwork, to float in the palm of one's hand.

Snow—melting in a warm Hawaiian hand. Coxe.

Thompson hired him on his return up the Columbia River, "a powerful well-made Sandwich Islander". Familiar only with his island, he kept expecting the river to end.

"The first shower of snow he was for some time catching in his hand, and before he could satisfy his curiosity it was melted. The next morning thin ice was formed, which he closely examined in his hand, but like the snow it also melted into water, and he was puzzled how the snow and ice could become water, but the great mountains soon settled his mind, where all became familiar to him."

My daughter and I walk past two boys catching snowflakes on their sleeves, towards a man and a woman under an umbrella. An elderly couple. Are they lighting a cigarette? No—he's doing up the top button of her coat. Tenderness. The snow brings it on.

Snow falls on the blue towel on the line. Four o'clock is whiter than three.

All the clotheslines come forward, overlined by snow, a chaotic, crazy background extending from every floor of every building—across.

When we bring the background forward shy images appear, wall-flowers and quiet animals. David Thompson was a reticent man and mapped a reticent country. Elsewhere I learn that he married Charlotte Small, a girl of fourteen, half-Cree, and with her had thirteen children. "My lovely wife," he calls her in a single reference later deleted from the final version of his *Travels*.

He barely mentions his private life. In one exception he describes how one of his horses nearly crushed his children to death on June 19th, 1808. Its load "badly put on, which I mistook for viciousness, I shot him on the spot and rescued my little ones." The incident reveals all the emotion otherwise only suggested by the careful tone, so nearly sensual in its appreciation of everything that touched his life.

"Of all furs the fur of the hare is the warmest; we place pieces of it in our mittens; the skin is too thin for any other purpose. . . ."

"All three men became snow blind, and for the last four days I had to lead them with a string tied to my belt, and . . . so completely blind that when they wished to drink of the little pools of melted snow, I had to put their hands in the water. . . ."

"The blue eye suffers first and most, the grey eye next, and the black eye the least; but none are exempt from snowblindness. . . ."

"The cold increases continually, with very little relaxation, the snow is now as dry as dust, about two feet in depth, it adheres to nothing, we may throw a gun into it and take it up as free of snow, as if in the air. . . ."

He was fourteen years old when he arrived on the shores of Hudson Bay. An apprentice clerk in the fur trade, he had been put into a charity school at the age of seven, his father having died a pauper when he was two. From seventeen to twenty he lived on the banks of the Saskatchewan River, for one whole winter in the tent of a Piegan chief. At nineteen he began to keep a notebook.

When he arrived in Canada in 1784, almost all of north-western America was a blank on the world map. He filled it in. "The greatest land geographer the British race has produced."

Pious, permeated with the Bible, monogamous, private. Inspired. A prodigious memory, an exquisite eye for detail. His *Travels* catch his thoughts at the moment of thinking and present all he sees in a style that's graceful and sweeping and "live".

"Almost the whole of these extensive countries were denuded of the beaver, the natives became poor . . . and in this state remain, and probably forever."

At the end of his life Thompson went bankrupt in eastern Ontario, "reduced to surveying city streets and private lots in order to barely live." At the age of seventy-three he was paid a piddling 150 pounds by the Canadian government for a complete, updated collection of his maps. Three years later, in 1846, he watched as the British government, deaf to all his entreaties and without a struggle, turned over the Oregon territory to the United States.

He spent the next five years writing his *Travels* and the following six years sick and nearly blind, so impoverished by his sons' debts and his own helplessness that he finally had to sell his instruments and pawn his coat. He died—his *Travels* unfinished—at the age of eighty-seven in 1857. His wife died three months later. They were buried on Mount Royal in a grave unmarked until J.B. Tyrrell, another geographer, put up a monument in 1927.

Beaver

For Canada, always ambivalent about itself, the national symbol is fitting, faintly ludicrous, certainly sad. Beaver, pussy. Where did that use of beaver come from?

In October 1797, Thompson walked over a beaver dam a mile long and saw "clusters of beaver houses like miniature villages," fifty-two in number. Halfway across the dam he came upon an old Indian, "his arms folded across his breast, with a pensive countenance, looking at the beaver swimming in the water, and carrying their winter's provisions to their houses. His form was tall and erect, his hair almost white. . . . He invited us to pass the night at his tent which was close by; the sun was low, and we accepted the offer."

That night they sat outside around the fire "and after smoking awhile, conversation came on." The Indian told Thompson that beaver had once been an ancient people and had lived on land. Always beaver, not humans, they had been wise and powerful, unmenaced by other animals or man, until in some way unknown to him they had angered the Great Spirit. As punishment He drove them into the water "and there let them live, still to be wise but without power."

The Indian told Thompson that the Great Spirit was angry with the beaver once again, and had revealed the secret of its destruction: castoreum, the thick liquid in the animal's scent glands, beaten up with green aspen buds and spread on short bruised willowsticks. The sticks were placed a foot beyond steel traps. "We are now killing the beaver without any labour."

Such a female fate, to be trapped by desire and worn as a fur coat.

Snow negates things. It covers them over.

Fur is what we negate. The animal. Women who hang beautiful, empty, lonely.

Women on Hangers

In the cupboard, blouses retain the smell of beautiful days (as a man who wore shaving lotion once remained on me). Imprisoned in the dark, they remember.

I look down and notice for the first time that Cathy wears four rings. Only her hands are visible one floor below as she hangs out her laundry.

Cathy is afraid of the subway and can't drive. Yesterday she went as a chaperone with her daughter's school to see the Statue of Liberty. It was *beautiful*, she said. She didn't climb to the top, though. Her hips wouldn't fit.

Her teenage daughter leans out the window. Down the street another girl leans out and, accompanying a cassette, sings into the street—sibilance. Her S's travel farther than she.

In our increasingly yellow cocoons we approach spring. Sealed off, isolated, women cushion their arms with pillows when they lean out the window.

In Ezra Pound's *Cathay* I come across his lines about the sun and moon always moving in search of a soft seat. Pound went mad on air, women come unpinned.

"I have no family here," Clara tells me.

"You came by yourself from Italy?"

"By myself. I was twenty years old."

"An arranged marriage?"

"Yes. Arranged." She shakes her head, her eyes soft with the imminent possibility of weeping.

"Awful," she says. "I'd never recommend it, not even to my worst enemy."

Two children in less than two years, she lived on the third floor, couldn't go out for a quart of milk unless she took both with her. So tired that once when she was nursing the second baby she felt him sliding out of her arms, powerless to hold him any longer.

"I had no one," she says.

Your husband, I want to ask—where was he?

Laura tells me. My daughter and I are in the backyard, Laura raises the window, rosary in hand. I count the rhine-stones in her glasses while I listen.

"She was so pretty when she came over," says Laura. "And thin," holding up her finger to demonstrate. "With red cheeks," and she pinches her own. "They were so mean to her."

"Her husband?"

"And her mother-in-law. They hit her all the time. The mother-in-law still lives right there above them, she's 103 years old. She never goes outside, you'll never see her outside."

Clara—Clelia. "But no one could pronounce it," implying with a look that no one wanted to.

* * *

Washing on the line. After two days of rain, the only life in the streets.

I listen to the mourning doves. Wait for the light to be just so—before snapping a photo. I want to remember this scene, I like it so much.

Sal did a wash this morning. It was hanging on the line when I looked out at 6:45, the first one he's done in three and a half months. Eighteen shirts and one pair of pants, the shirts like low-income butterflies: bright yellow, purple and white, pink and red, pink and black. I remember seeing him walk down the street in the yellow one.

I wonder if he ever looks over here—his windows face ours. I wonder if he sees me drinking this cup of coffee.

Sal—the name Jack Kerouac gave himself in *On the Road*. My appetite awakened by his, I make an apple pie and eat it with vanilla ice-cream as he did going west. "I knew it was nutritious, and it certainly was delicious."

Sal comes out. He carries a plastic shopping bag as always, but a trench coat has replaced his winter jacket. White moustache, white hair, yellowish streaks. Unshaven, shy.

His mailbox is beside ours.

We approach at the mailman's speed, my daughter's tiny steps, his house-by-house stops, and arrive at Sal's perfume: aftershave despite the lack of one. He asks the mailman if it's there, and the mailman sorts the mail. "No."

"The cheque's not there? That surprises me. It usually comes on the third, and it didn't come yesterday either."

My daughter and I go inside.

The landlord comes out of Sal's house, turns around in the doorway and shakes his finger at him. It must be the rent.

* * *

I saw the Ecuadorean woman this morning. She walked by

dressed in fake fur. The one who's beaten all the time, says Clara.

I said to Laura last night, "I feel so sorry for Hedda Nussbaum."

Her picture had been in the papers all week. A writer of children's books, a former editor at Random House. Her six-year-old daughter was found beaten to death, Hedda herself was "black and blue" when she and her husband were brought into court.

"Do you? I don't feel a bit sorry."

"Why not?"

"I don't have any sympathy for a woman who doesn't defend her children."

"But she was frightened, beaten."

"She could have done like any other woman."

And that's when Laura told me that thirty-five years ago she got a court order against her husband.

On another occasion Clara was there too, and we were discussing divorce, which they both oppose. Clara said, "This world isn't meant for joy, it's meant for suffering."

Lawnchairs on the sidewalk, tattoos on men. Women take the air by sitting on the sidewalk; men remain inside watching television, their faces inked with pale blue light.

Clara said of the Ecuadorean woman, "When she was pregnant he beat her all the time. Their bed must be right above mine, it's awful."

Pregnant with the little girl who was killed a month ago. Their car rolled over an embankment into the river, the others escaped but the little girl drowned.

"Her body was black in the coffin, all black."

Beaten since before she was born.

* * *

Why does it make me so uneasy to put clothes into drawers? Especially my daughter's. The suggestion of finality. The end of their life on the line.

We've come back after a few days away, and the closed smell is overpowering. The end of motion—a spillage of bags, diapers, food, toys. A stopping short that makes me almost nauseated.

The familiar deadened by our absence, we enter our own absence and it's all too familiar. Domestic violence of loneliness, smack of isolation. The future—waiting for us— in a drawer.

"Every time I think of that it makes me feel sad," Alec says on the phone, "a little sick inside."

I know the question without hearing it. When are you going back to Mexico?

"I don't know," he answers. "In the fall, I guess." But he sounds unconvinced, depressed that it won't happen sooner, might not happen even then.

It's been a year and a half since we left, since we packed and unpacked, opened and closed drawers on a difficult ending and a difficult beginning.

The picture haunts me. The first picture I saw of Hedda. Lips puffed out, nose broken, flattened, bandaged. Her eyes, all of her, beyond crying. The face of a cavewoman beaten backwards into some awful misery. And her husband beside her—strong, vigorous, husky.

Each had been charged with attempted murder, assault, and endangerment of the welfare of their child, who lay in hospital, unconscious, blood on her brain, having been found naked, "unusually thin" and not breathing after Hedda called emergency because her daughter "had choked on some vegetables."

Hedda's face stares ahead/down at nothing. Chalky.

As though flour has been poured over her blackened features.

One of her neighbours said, "I've been here in the building thirteen years and he's been beating her thirteen years."

"I got a court order," Laura told me, "against my husband. My son was about six then."

"And he stopped?"

"Oh yeah—they put him on probation for six months."

Louis. The man she's been married to for forty-seven years. Three years ago he fell down the stairs and went into a coma for three months. When he woke up Laura brought him home. They said he would live six months, but here he is. Laura changes his diapers, hoists him in and out of bed, never goes out except to buy food or go to church.

Just as she sits down to eat, he gets a gleam in his eye. "Laura, I want a glass of water." Or, "Laura, I just did it."

And she wheels him into the bedroom, lifts him onto the bed, wipes the shit off his frail haunches and puts on a fresh diaper. The stink fills the apartment. Then she wheels him back to the table, stuffs his pills into his mouth, crams them in with her fingers so that he almost chokes.

Cathy tells me that all last summer Louis accused Laura of having an affair, because she would go out in the evening and stand in the street to get some air.

An affair with air.

* * *

Sal—six windows. Four of them covered with permanently drawn yellow blinds, two with curtains and plastic, but perhaps some light penetrates. I've never seen him in any of the windows, and I've seen a light on in only one.

"No," Laura tells me, "he never raises his blinds

except in the summer when it gets really hot."

"He's in there all day? With the blinds drawn?"

"Oh no. He hangs out at that little restaurant on Graham Avenue beside ABC Bargains. He has a friend there, Wally, the busboy—or busman."

Sal smiled today. He said hello as I lifted my daughter's stroller into the street. He has never offered a greeting before.

We watch the progress of Clara's magnolia tree. I open the windows hoping for fragrance. It should be an orange scent.

Dark/dim/bright. The motion from inside the bud to its pinkish white surface. My daughter is asleep in the far room, Alec is sick in the middle room and I'm here, in the kitchen, with a cup of coffee and rain on the magnolia, afraid the blossoms will be disturbed before they open, disturbed but opening in the peacefulness, the quiet. My spot.

Magnolia blossoms tilt towards the east. Last night I went to the Chinese grocer's, where the young cashier rubs her fingers on half a lemon before riffling open the plastic bags. Stopping there or simply passing gives me such pleasure: oranges, red peppers, flowers illuminated by lightbulbs under an awning.

Korean, says Alec.

Never mind. Cathay.

"Now I know why I've been thinking about Billie Holiday the last couple of days," says Alec as we listen to her on the radio. "I was thinking about the interview they played last year; it's been a year."

An interesting sense of time—to have the buds remind him of Billie, reminded because the radio remembers.

I lean out the window into the perfume of clothes,

Cathy's down below: soap rises, sudsy magnolia. They play a rehearsal session from mid-August, 1955. So drunk. Impossible to make out what she says.

    Snapping her fingers.

    Magnolia stems.

    She would be seventy-two.

We talk about whether her voice was better in the thirties and forties, or in the fifties. Whether it was better when it was ragged and haunted but more mature, or younger, fresher, with a happier beat. Alec prefers the older, I the younger. More feeling, he says. But there was plenty of feeling before, and less pain.

    She died at the age of forty-four. 1959.

* * *

Still life—lips. Except when they move: the uncoloured lips of the homeless grey-haired woman, pressed together in sudden laughter suddenly over, tremors that pass uncensored over the face of a newborn, reading her future.

    Clara sweeps brown withered petals off the sidewalk. Her husband never comes outside. I went to retrieve a towel blown into their yard, and knocked on the apartment door. He opened it. "Ask my wife," and he indicated the apartment one door over.

    As if to summarize her whole life, Clara never hangs out washing unless it's bound to rain. Again today— overcast, an 80 percent chance of rain, and her line is full.

I fold sheets, reminded of my mother folding anger into herself. On hot summer days she would continue to cook with transparent good humour, as though dressed for the occasion. Her anger—hard stones under an inch of clear

water.   Or better—light on the other side of clothes: clear,
barely impeded, lowering so that it comes through sleeves.

Evening light as low as cuffs.

My daughter whines and tugs at my leg until I swear
at her and walk away (a clothesline walking away from
clothes) into the far room, where I shut the door and huddle
against the wall for a few minutes.   It only makes her worse,
of course.

Cold today.   The magnolia—thin.   The tips of Clara's
stockings on the line; a neighbourhood down at the heel.

Sal stands on the sidewalk, Cathy leans out the
second-floor window.

"Okay, I'll phone," he says. (He uses the pay phone
on Graham Avenue.)

"Thank you, Catherine."

No one else uses her full name.   He is so bashful, so
eager, not to please, exactly, just not to offend.   He closes the
gate and it doesn't catch.   Cathy calls after him to close it and
he does so hastily, apologetically, with infinite care.

The man who has been carrying things out of Sal's house (at
the moment a standing tin closet) has a mouth like a sucked-
in waist, and a waist like a soft, full mouth.   I go downstairs
and find Laura and Clara in lawnchairs on the sidewalk.

"What's happened to Sal?" I ask.

"Gone.   Moved out."

"Where?"

"A furnished room in Greenpoint."

"And all his things?"

"They're clearing it all away now—he left everything behind almost."

The mover is Wally, the busman.   He brings out a big
box tied with a string which breaks.   Records spill out.

Broadway musicals, the theme music to "Ben Casey", *Oklahoma !*—

"He was quite a dancer," Laura says. "Oh yes. And he sewed all his own costumes. He couldn't read or write—his sister told me—but if somebody had picked him up, some designer, he could have made a fortune."

"He danced? Where? For money?"

"He used to dance in those places, you know, dressed up."

"Like a woman?"

"Yeah. He made the most beautiful things, sequins and appliqué. He had hands of gold. Thirteen— fifteen years he's been here. He had a companion, Al, but he died."

"What's in that wooden box?" she asks Wally.

"His brushes."

"Oh—he was a painter too," Laura tells me. "Beautiful things."

Lowering her voice, "Al had a nervous breakdown. Such nice boys. I call them boys, I'm old enough to be their mother. They were together since they were kids, and they never gave us a bit of trouble. Never brought anybody back there, never."

"When did Al die?"

"Let's see. My Lorraine—may she rest—died two months ago, and my sister five months ago. Seven months ago."

"Why did Sal leave all his things behind?"

"Oh, he'll just have one room."

Clara adds, "When the husband dies, you know. . . . Do you understand what I mean?"

* * *

There are two styles, pinning by the shoulders or by the feet.

The Asian woman who lives two houses over pins her clothes by their small bound feet.

Connected by clothes, by the disarming intimacy of ragged underwear between dilapidated buildings. Beautiful connections of colour, shape, motion, in the sun.

In clothesline stories, as in radio stories, bodies are invisible; we have to imagine. Clara's bloomers have holes, Cathy's towels are frayed.

Women in this neighbourhood live taped lives, the same every day, over and over again.

Going live. Going taped. Going bandaged.

The tone of trapped things (Billie's tone) forms the music.

Back to Yellowknife

I follow Raggedy Ass Lane through Willow Flats. Ravens are about. It's cold, and they talk very little. This is the first time I've been here in ten years, and I'm on the radio again.

The snow isn't deep. Yellowknife never gets much snow, just enough to remain white, dry, beautiful. Enough to satisfy eyes tired from looking through a dirty Brooklyn window. I haven't been here for ten years.

My friend Sheila's house is in Willow Flats. Light pours in through her windows and falls on the twenty-year-old jade plant, the vase of silk flowers on the table, the I Ching. I handle the coins, old and worn, the pattern rubbed off the backs of two of them, and talk about the Arctic going backwards to warmth. Millions of years ago, in a subtropical paradise, swamp cypress and dawn redwood grew here—trees which now grow only in China.

She tells me that as a child she realized she would go backwards through life: she would have to grow up in order to express all the things she knew as a child.

We throw the coins six times. "The Receptive, which moves downward, stands above; the Creative, which moves upward, is below. This hexagram belongs to the first month (February-March), at which time the forces of nature prepare the new spring."

It's February. The coldest weather is over. The days are already long.

An image occurs to me of three footprints in the snow. The first one fresh, made only yesterday; the second half-filled with snow, its contours rounded; and the third, older still, softened even more, the outline of the foot simply a hollow, and in that hollow, soft blue light. This suggests an advance that's a retreat, and a retreat that brings one home to oneself.

Ten years ago I sat on our deck facing Back Bay and Louise sat next door facing the road. She sent a long stream of spit into the grass.

Louise must have been about sixty then. She wore mukluks, low rubbers, ankle socks, thick brown stockings, a skirt, a blue jacket. Her teeth bothered her and she sucked them. Every so often she would pick up blowing garbage in her yard, walk over to the line that divided the two lots and drop it on our side.

Those were the summers of ravens' wings outside the window and sled-dogs down behind the house. Six of them were tied to the willows, they wore the ground bare.

Light took over. At night we pulled down the blinds in the bedroom, ordered from the catalogue with too-small measurements, and light poured through on either side. The plants in the window were bleached, the windows were old and wouldn't open.

The windows looked out onto the backyard across the lack of grass and the garden (in the end, only cabbages) to Back Bay and the opposite shore—the rocks and ravens, the small old graveyard hidden from view, and Giant Mine. Louise's shack was on the right. Ten-foot willows lined the water's edge, some of them burned and still not growing after the fire of the summer before.

Louise was prodding the ground with her cane. She called out to me, then pointed with her cane, and I saw the burnt grass and realized she'd said fire. The grass was black right to the edge of her shack and in the dip behind.

We always thought about fire. Coming down Franklin Avenue towards Old Town, around the base of the rock, alongside the float planes and over the little bridge to Latham Island, we looked to see if the house had burned down, the wood so dry and the wind blowing. Louise's second outhouse lay on its side in the dip.

Louise in her bandanna, her white cane. One day she came outside with a can of paint and sat down on the spot of grass in front of her door; green and soft, almost mossy, the seagulls liked it. She opened the can, dipped her brush and painted the cane completely white. A few days later a nurse parked her car on the edge of the road and carried a new black cane down to Louise's door.

Her nephew, Andrew, often sat beside her. Lopsided Andrew. People said he threw himself in front of cars in order to collect insurance money. He cleaned fish in a basin, then rolled his pant legs above his knees and washed his legs.

Ten years later the shack is still here, but Louise isn't. Boards are nailed across the windows.

On Frame Lake, frozen over and indistinguishable from the rest of the snowy country except by its flatness under a pale blue sky, I remember a summer's day when Keith and David and I canoed on the lake. Blue dragonflies lit on our shoulders, our arms, our hands.

Northern explorers wrote about kinds of cold, ways of dying, sources of unexpected warmth. And always that haunting image of a place that used to be warm. Imagine the delicate growth, the soft ferns, the tender mouths of subtropical animals.

"The fur countries", they called them. And in the same breath spoke of memory. Samuel Hearne, it was said, like all residents of the fur countries, had an excellent memory.

Is there a qualitative difference between northern memory and southern? Between the imprint of heat and the imprint of cold? Reading about Fort Reliance, I remember it. The flat, almost parklike bench of land, the crumbled stone chimneys, the tinkling of ice candles at the edge of the shore. Lichen crunched underfoot.

As part of their "fort", Captain Back's men built an observatory with "four windows of moose-skin parchment with a small pane of glass in each." They took the temperatures of animals, birds, fish, trees and earth. On October 25th, 1833, when the air temperature was 12 degrees, the air close to the ground was 16 degrees warmer and the centre of a fir tree 4 degrees warmer than that. On January 7th, 1834, when it was 27 below, the breast of a white partridge registered 110 degrees and a red pole 99. That summer a thermometer placed through the ball wound of a musk-ox, blood oozing from the heart, stopped rising at 104 degrees.

This must be one of the qualities of a northern memory: the attention to degrees, to any change however slight.

I jot down ideas for interviews: someone who grades fur—knows the quality—a good year; the people who come and go in the store at Nahanni Butte, in the café at Fort Liard, in the school at Trout Lake; the nature of a winter's day in a small settlement. The trouble is, people are quiet.

The plane is four seats wide. I move forward away from the freezing draft which comes through the door, and towards the stewardess who says "doggone" and gives two Dene kids can after can of Coke.

We land in Fort Simpson, a wooded island in the Mackenzie River. In the hotel two waiters sit at a table reading Chinese newspapers and eating with forks. (On the plane from New York to Yellowknife my seatmate was Asian; my first cabdriver was Asian. He used to live in Kerry, he told me. After a moment I got it. Calgary.)

In the morning the wind howls, and snow blankets the window. I pull on my boots—something hard. An orange pip shakes out onto the floor.

Outside, winds are fifty miles an hour. Huge chunks of ice have been thrown up along the river-bank, and it's virtually impossible to walk. A telephone repairman stops and offers me a ride. I'm going to Gus Kraus's, I say, and he takes me there.

Gus is lying on the sofa. An old trapper, confined by ill health, crazy from confinement but gracious even so. He raises his grey face off his grey pillow and welcomes me. He used to live at the hot springs in the Nahanni Valley, a lush mountain area of thick birches and soft grass. In the winter the floor of his cabin was so warm from the springs below that he walked in bare feet. He bathed in the springs: "green grass all winter long . . . you used to come along there and your feet were cold, just stand on the rocks, the rocks were nice and dry, big boulders just standing there. Heck, in no time your feet were nice." He had a garden and grew melons.

From the fact of the hot springs came the legend of a northern valley filled with orange groves. One of the pips got into my boot.

* * *

Everywhere in Trout Lake marten pelts are piled high, and so are the skinned bodies. The bodies are a dull pinkish red, very small. Skinned lynx are larger, the size of big cats, and slender.

Emily Jumbo skins several marten. She pulls the pelt away from the flesh, stretches it, rolls it in her hands. The inside of the pelt is almost elastic. White with intricate tracings of red veins. It feels moist. Soft.

This gentle skinning. Quiet sound of a knife breaking through skin, a slight thump.

"In 1827, the shipment of trade goods received at Fort Simpson from the main depot of York Factory included: 15 crimson and scarlet belts, 50 common-coloured belts, several kilos of beads, over 150 blankets, a dozen shaving boxes, 2 dozen horn combs, 60 powder horns, clothes of various sorts, 8 bags flour, 2 kegs butter, 6 cases guns, 9 bags shot, 16 kegs gunpowder. The fur returns from the Mackenzie River District for the same year totalled close to 13,000 pounds, and included over 4800 beaver, 6900 marten, 33,700 muskrat."

I finger an old newspaper clipping, yellow now, something I've saved for twelve years. It's one of Joe Punch's stories about Trout Lake. "It's been quite awhile, since I've last wrote for we are all fine, and its been a little busy Summer time, for we had tourists once awhile." Joe Punch used to write his "Notes from Trout Lake" for *The News of the North*. "There some boys here, are working with this Cat D8 so there some community jobs. Like moving the teacher's house close to the school, and a new garbage pit, hauling logs for to build housing for some family, like I mean this new comer, Mr. and Mrs. Philip Edda and daughter Loretta for they stayed here since mid July 1975, for they all really like to stay here for they say its lot better than Nahanni Butte, for they came from."

Joe Punch is short and stocky with a squashed face, very talkative. One of his daughters watches *Terminator* on the VCR while her baby sleeps in a small flannel hammock.

Joe talks about the caribou and fish they've taken this winter, and about the price of electricity now that power lines run into the settlement; Trout Lake has sixty-three people.

Joe takes me to see the chief. We walk on pathways between houses. It's very warm, a chinook has swept in, and water drips from eaves. Occasionally it splashes our faces.

The chief's granddaughter plays with a dead rabbit on the floor while Joe translates for the chief. Since I barely understand Joe, I don't understand the chief. But it's a necessary and pleasant courtesy.

Later the teacher makes tea for me, and I think about him—his situation alone—as we fly out of Trout Lake over the scrub spruce and poplar, away from the cluster of log houses, a settlement without roads or mail. I think about the white anthropologist who arrived in 1980 and stayed: three children, blood on her hands from cleaning fish, greying hair, overweight; her husband's shy, pocked face.

* * *

In Nahanni Butte, twelve-year-old children have written perfect haiku. I copy them down off the classroom wall.

> *the day I stepped out*
> *everything on earth looked white*
> *in June colour comes out.*

> *the mountains are white*
> *and covered with soft snowflakes.*
> *Wind blowing harshly.*

> *on a snowy day*
> *the snowflakes were going down*
> *very very slow*

the lake still is cold
the pike leaps to the evening sun
through ash-flecked snow

On the school windowsill, plasticine skidoos are lined up, so finely crafted the park warden recognizes the make of each one. Drawings on the wall use perspective, something the children know instinctively, never having been taught.

At eleven at night the full moon falls on log cabins and snow. Who is the last to go to sleep, I ask. Who is the first to rise? Trying, in twenty-four hours, to get a sense of the settlement and communicate it on the radio.

Outside there is nothing to be read except the late-night stillness, late-night beauty, all the lives quietly out of reach.

Existence is so precarious. Or rather, feeling alive. That is so precarious. Hours go by and not another vehicle. I drive the Mackenzie Highway in a four-wheel truck, and frequently feel the wheels slide, and slow down. I keep looking in the mirror. Or rather, when I look, I keep seeing an older face. People say I'm thinner.

In the Fort Simpson airport a photograph of the queen hangs on the wall. She looks her age.

I call Alec. My daughter answers, and talks for a long time while the operator keeps asking her to get her mother. Then Alec comes on and accepts the collect call. Amazing to hear her voice, at once more mature and more childish, higher-pitched yet a fuller vocabulary.

Alec teases me about driving on ice rivers. Urges me to have fun. Are you? he asks.

I'm in a strange mood, I say. And try to explain being out of touch with myself, and out of touch with the north. But it's an airport phone, my daughter is talking in the background.

The day I leave Fort Simpson and go back to Yellowknife, the Chinese leave too. After seven years they're going to Vancouver, driving overnight.

I look out at the snow, and write with a green felt-pen. Several plants sit in the window. Spindly, large. Lush by northern standards.

Where are the Chinese now, I wonder. In Kerry?

Bob takes me to Detah by dogteam—a snow boat over snow waves as the toboggan bounces up and down on the trail. The dogs reach to the side and swipe mouthfuls of snow while Bob runs alongside. (Smell of breakfast orange on my fingertips. Someone tells me the Inuit word for tree is the Japanese word for fire. Inuktitut has many words with an oriental cast.)

Sheila serves Labrador tea in Chinese bowls, and we eat with chopsticks—chicken, green pods, black beans. The house is cool and she doesn't mind. She gives me a big sweater to pull over the one I'm wearing. Her house has two rooms and she lives alone.

"Do you get lonely?" I ask.

"No. I don't. I seem to have the right amount of solitude and the right number of friends."

The last person I thought would stay. "You used to say there was nothing beautiful to look at, nothing to rest your eyes on. Do you remember?"

She shakes her head. "I suppose I did think that."

A year ago she wrote me a letter about her winter of 40 below outside and 40 below inside. And then something "oriental?" happened, and she began to see paintings everywhere. Her paintings are tiny landscapes suffused with colour and light.

She looks older. Like everyone in Yellowknife, she

has dry skin.

One day I learned why the seagulls flew down to that spot of grass in front of Louise's door, and why the spot of grass was so green. She brought out her pans and knocked the leftover food onto the ground.

David stood behind our house and took a photograph of the field aglow with arctic cotton, the three shacks next to the water, the bay beyond. While summer lasted David stayed up till two in the morning, then got up again at six, poured himself half a cup of coffee and sniffed the aroma till he left for work. He never could drink coffee, it made him jump out of his skin.

From Sheila I learn that Louise is in an old folk's home uptown. Has been for a couple of years. Andrew is still about. Whenever he sees Sheila he asks for a dollar, she gives him one and he asks for another. She has a soft spot for Andrew—the engaging grin, an outsider among outsiders.

I close the door behind me, bang it, and hear the window rattle, and the ravens, four of them, around garbage on the road. Tracks remain in the snow for months. A pair of false teeth skitters into the yard.

"When he begins a journey over open terrain," I read in a book about the north, an Eskimo "marks the angle of the wind and checks his bearing periodically by glancing at the fur of his parka rim, at its alignment with the breeze."

The plane takes off and I look back and down through fur—my own parka hood.

* * *

March 20th. Back in Brooklyn. When I went to bed a light dusting of snow had fallen, and the neighbour across the street—from some warm country—had shovelled and swept painstakingly yet curiously. He followed no pattern, no efficient method of removal, but pushed his shovel in curves over and over again, leaving the sidewalk immaculate where he worked, but always partially covered in snow no matter how long he worked. I decided he was a little crazy. Then reflected that if this was his first snowfall, or even his fourth, such erratic behaviour might be natural.

I realize now why initially I felt so comfortable here. With my view out the window, of Clara's garden, the poor backyards, the laundry, all of it down at the heel but cozy somehow, and the absence of trees—it reminded me of Yellowknife. I bring in a towel from the clothesline, and smell Stan: the fresh heady smell of dog outside all day, fur ironed by cold, metallic sky.

Is it snow I'm smelling on the towel? Was it snow I smelled on Stan?

On the barrens our canoe had a memory. It was made of a material that returned to its original shape after any sort of impact. Indented by the smell of snow.

Simultaneous Translations

Smell of tobacco and basil simultaneously on my fingertips, green and dry. Hector left his pack of Camels on the record player and I smoke one by an open window, reduced to sneakiness, expanded by smoke.

Every so often I think of Georgia O'Keeffe's beautiful hands holding a stone as she walked around her garden, taking the same number of turns every day. She had a pile of small round stones, and each time she passed she would pick one up and put it down in a new place, forming a new pile for the next day. In this way she walked undistracted by counting.

Simultaneous translation, stone on bone through the skin of connection.

I read "the bells ring" and they do.

I open Barbara's book and she calls.

An ice cube cracks and my thumb splits.

In simultaneous translation the voice of one climate runs under the voice of another, and the two become a third whose strands are still decipherable—as hot and cold—but speaking to each other. Less to each other than to us. They couple, become intimate, melt together but still exist, as in any good love story.

Every morning I throw a white sheet over the small

oak table, pull the rocking-chair into the middle of the room and spray the plants until they drip. To be inside summer when it's winter, surrounded by green and reminded of snow, next to a table draped as if for winter, yet feeling the brush of fern fronds on my hand.

In the recess that contains my desk, David's photograph of Yellowknife hangs alongside photographs of muskoxen, caribou, a snow fence on Great Slave Lake. The wall next to the recess is Mexican: a bark painting, papier-mâché birds, lacquered animals, death toys on a shelf higher up. Of these two halves the northern is almost entirely black and white, the Mexican, colour.

I unbalance the balance. I glue David's fluorescent pink and orange hearts and his photograph of the religious procession in Zinacantán to a piece of paper, and stick the paper under the edge of the frame that holds his photograph of Yellowknife. This adds colour to the half of the room that has been black and white, and adds Mexico to the half that has been northern. Now the south outweighs the north, although the fact that his hearts are broken perhaps outweighs everything.

Caribou arrange themselves on a sandbank around low willows, their formation determined by hunger and the desire for company.

On the barrens we ate strawberries: our first campsite, strawberries and fresh cream. Later, warm wind came off the sand as we pulled the canoes over ice; cool air came onshore when we sat on the sand.

Lives are recorded on each other, and we transcribe them. We lie down on the grass and when we get up our bodies retain the imprint of grass and twigs. Just as arctic coal retains the imprint of tropical leaves, and snow the weight of a footstep.

I was reading Cinderella to my daughter and remembered that in the original tale the slipper was made of fur. Only in translation did it become glass. *Vair* to *verre*, fur to glass. The smallest slip and we enter an entirely different world.

Alec's sprained arm is raised and resting on a pillow. Almost imperceptible, the breeze from the ceiling fan. His waking.

He can barely move his wrist. The breeze is like that. Like the smell of coffee inside a refrigerator.

Samuel Hearne wrote that when otters are pursued in the woods "where the snow is always light and deep", they dive down under it, "but are easily traced by the motion of the snow above them, and soon overtaken."

Snow translates fur, a blanket the body underneath it—that slight curve under which so much is concealed. Lift a single vowel and chine becomes China.

A chine is a backbone or spine. To chine: to cut along or across the backbone (through fur to China). To open, germinate, burst into bloom, as these connections burst open tying furs to the orient. Hard-chined boats—York boats, thirty to forty feet long—replaced canoes for carrying furs.

Within one word exists the whole story of cutting, flowering, furs in full bloom, a chined boat cutting across a body of language to Cathay.

My deodorant smells of cloves.

* * *

In the fall fig trees are wrapped in tarpaper, or buried if they're young. "They dig a hole," says Clara, "like a grave, then bend the tree over into the hole and cover it with dirt and leaves. To keep them warm."

Warmth is found in unexpected places. In the Arctic the temperature among the dead leaves of a saxifrage or inside a cushion of dark mosses is twenty to forty degrees warmer than the ambient air.

Cinderella's foot was a warm paw, a wild animal that disappeared at midnight and reappeared the next night, in the way animals once had of becoming human.

Snow leaves the north and arrives in Havana as talcum powder under an arm.

Fur produces long travels which bring us to new forms of cold—the chilly spot on my daughter's stomach after she holds a glass of ice water against it.

Loud music from the back. They're gutting Sal's house. The yellow blinds have been taken away, and a radio blasts in the open doorway.

Clara fries zucchini flowers into pendulous pancakes. Delicious. August. Days are as long as the shaved portion of a young neighbour's legs; night as short as her dark upper thighs.

I sit on the fire escape, and watch the moon. Bingo players come out of St. Nicholas church about ten. The neighbour one house over pulls in clothes and hangs out more.

In the heat I remember things about Havana: the thermos of ice water in our room, the soap that stayed soft for ever, that vivid week of heat, heated argument, gentle decay. We sat in rocking-chairs which created a breeze, lattice-work windows offered more.

Slowly I'm surrounding myself with things I had rejected. I take out all the Mexican objects I had stored away in boxes, all the things that made me feel inadequate and drab. I translate the south, and the south translates me.

I meant to write more so and wrote more snow.

When off season is in season. Memory—all the previous seasons present in the mind.

The rain almost touches me—a narrow roof above. Finally does and I come inside off the fire escape, but not before feeling through the screen the heat of the house on my right thigh, cooling evening on my left. From a long day of heat into grey evening, owl. Coming to my senses, coming home.

We nail a lacquered Mexican shelf to the kitchen wall, and on it place a bird-covered candlestick (*árbol de la vida,* tree of life) and a small pot of ivy. Above them a mirror hangs in a gaily lacquered frame.

I search in my mind for something northern to include. A feather? A stone? Then move slightly to the right and notice the reflection in the mirror—the refrigerator across the room.

A shrine, then, to north and south.

Lachine was the starting point, that wistful fur outpost eight miles west of Montreal. The end was Cathay— where furs were prized and ivory made into snowballs.

In between . . . ourselves, of course. Looking for Cathay and finding fur. Looking for fur and finding various Cathays. As though we're off the map, casting about between climates of love.

Sources

Back, George. *Narrative of the Arctic Land Expedition to the Mouth of the Great Fish River.* Philadelphia, 1836.

Champlain, Samuel de. *Works.* Ed. H. P. Biggar. Toronto: Champlain Society. 1922-36.

Danckaerts, Jasper. *Journal of Jasper Danckaerts.* New York: Scribner's, 1913.

Hall, Charles Francis. *Arctic Researches and Life Among the Esquimaux.* New York: Harper, 1874.

Hearne, Samuel. *Journey from Prince of Wales Fort in Hudson's Bay to the Northern Ocean.* Ed. J. B. Tyrrell. Toronto: Champlain Society, 1907-14.

Henry, Alexander. *Travels and Adventures in Canada and the Indian Territories.* Ed. James Bain. Toronto, 1901.

Innis, Harold. *The Fur Trade in Canada.* University of Toronto Press, 1970.

Lescarbot, Marc. *The History of New France,* Trans. and ed. W. L. Grant. Toronto: Champlain Society, 1907-14.

Loomis, Chauncey. *Weird and Tragic Shores. The Story of Charles Francis Hall.* New York: Knopf, 1971.

Mackenzie. Alexander. *Voyages from Montreal through the Continent of North America.* New York: New Amersterdam Book Co., 1902.

Morison, Samuel Eliot, *Samuel de Champlain, Father of New France.* Boston: Little, Brown, 1972.

Mowat, Farley. *Ordeal by Ice.* McClelland and Stewart, 1973.

———*The Polar Passion.* McClelland and Stewart, 1973.

Parkman, Franxis. *France and England in North America,* volume 1. The Library of America, 1983.

Thompson, David. *Narrative of his Explorations in Western Canada.* Ed. J.B. Tyrell, Toronto: Champlain Society, 1916.

———*Travels.* Ed. Victor Hopwood. MacMillan, 1971.

Thanks to The Indian Colonial Research Center in Old Mystic, Connecticut and to The New London County Historical society in New London, Connnecticut for access to their collections about Hannah (Tookoolito).